KANT'S
INTRODUCTION TO LOGIC,

AND HIS

ESSAY ON THE MISTAKEN SUBTILTY OF THE FOUR FIGURES:

TRANSLATED BY

THOMAS KINGSMILL ABBOTT, B. D.,

FELLOW AND TUTOR OF TRINITY COLLEGE, DUBLIN:

WITH

A FEW NOTES BY COLERIDGE.

PHILOSOPHICAL LIBRARY

NEW YORK

PREFATORY NOTE.

K ANT'S "LOGIC" was published in 1800. With the exception of the "Introduction" here translated, it consists of a Compendium of the ordinary School Logic, with occasional remarks. In fact, Kant in his Lectures used as a text-book a Compendium published by Meier (a disciple of the Wolffian school) in 1752. This he interleaved and annotated for his own use, and from these materials the "Logic" was, at Kant's instance, compiled by his pupil, Jäsche, afterwards professor at Dorpat.

The paging in the text is that of Rosenkranz (*Sämmtliche Werke*, Thl. 3).

The essay "On the Mistaken Subtilty of the Four Figures," was published in 1762 (*Werke*, Thl. 1).

The notes by COLERIDGE are extracted from his copy of Kant's "Logik" in the British Museum.

I have again to thank Professor SELSS for much kind help.

T. K. ABBOTT.

KANT'S INTRODUCTION TO LOGIC.

I.

CONCEPTION OF LOGIC.

EVERYTHING in nature, whether in the animate or inanimate world, takes place *according to rules*, although we do not always know these rules. Water falls according to laws of gravity, and in animals locomotion also takes place according to rules. The fish in the water, the bird in the air, moves according to rules. All nature, indeed, is nothing but a combination of phenomena which follow rules ; and *nowhere* is there *any irregularity*. When we think we find any such, we can only say that the rules are unknown.

The exercise of our own faculties takes place also according to certain rules, which we follow at first *unconsciously*, until by a long-continued use of our faculties we attain the knowledge of them, and at last make them so familiar, that it costs us much trouble to think of them *in abstracto*. Thus, *ex. gr.* general grammar is the form of language in general. One may speak, however, without knowing grammar, and he who speaks without knowing it has really a grammar, and speaks according to rules of which, however, he is not aware.

[170] Now, like all our faculties, the *understanding*, in particular, is governed in its actions by rules which we can investigate. Nay, the understanding is to be regarded as the source and faculty of conceiving rules in general. For just as the sensibility is the faculty of intuitions, so the understanding is the faculty of thinking, that is, of bringing the ideas of sense

under rules. It desires, therefore, to seek for rules, and is satisfied when it has found them. We ask, then, since the understanding is the source of rules, What rules does it follow itself? For there can be no doubt that we cannot think or use our understanding otherwise than according to certain rules. Now these rules, again, we may make a separate object of thought, that is, we can conceive them, *without their application*, or *in abstracto*. What now are these rules?

All rules which the understanding follows, are either *necessary* or *contingent*. The former are those without which no exercise of the understanding would be possible at all; the latter are those without which some certain definite exercise of the understanding could not take place. The contingent rules which depend on a definite object of knowledge are as manifold as these objects themselves. For example, there is an exercise of the understanding in mathematics, metaphysics, morals, &c. The rules of this special definite exercise of the understanding in these sciences are contingent, because it is contingent that I think of this or that object to which these special rules have reference.

If, however, we set aside all knowledge that we can only borrow from *objects*, and reflect simply on the exercise of the understanding in general, then we discover those rules which are absolutely necessary, independently of any particular objects of thought, because without them we cannot think at all. [171] These rules, accordingly, can be discerned *à priori*, that is, *independently of all experience*, because they contain merely the conditions of the use of the understanding in general, whether pure or empirical, without distinction of its objects. Hence, also, it follows that the universal and necessary laws of thought can only be concerned with its *form*, not in anywise with its *matter*. The science, therefore, which contains these universal and necessary laws is simply a science of the form of thought. And we can form a conception of the possibility of such a science, just as of a *universal grammar* which contains nothing beyond the mere form of language, without words, which belong to the matter of language.

This science of the necessary laws of the understanding and the reason generally, or, which is the same thing, of the mere form of thought generally, we call *Logic*.

Since Logic is a science which refers to all thought, without regard to objects which are the matter of thought, it must therefore be viewed—

1. as the *basis* of all other sciences, and the *propædeutic* of all employment of the understanding. But just because it abstracts altogether from objects—

2. it cannot be an *organon* of the sciences.

By an *organon* we mean an instruction how some particular branch of knowledge is to be attained. This requires that I already know the object of this knowledge which is to be produced by certain rules. An organon of the sciences is therefore not a mere logic, since it presupposes the accurate knowledge of the objects and sources of the sciences. [172] For example, mathematics is an excellent organon, being a science which contains the principles of extension of our knowledge in respect of a special use of reason. Logic, on the contrary, being the general propædeutic of every use of the understanding and of the reason, cannot meddle with the sciences, and anticipate their matter, and is therefore only a *universal Art of Reason* (*Canonica Epicuri*), the Art of making any branch of knowledge accord with the form of the understanding. Only so far can it be called an organon, one which serves not for the *enlargement*, but only for the *criticism and correction* of our knowledge.

3. Since Logic is a science of the necessary laws of thought, without which no employment of the understanding and the reason takes place, which consequently are the conditions under which alone the understanding can and should be consistent with itself—the necessary laws and conditions of its right use —Logic is therefore a *Canon*. And being a canon of the understanding and the reason, it cannot borrow any principles either from any science or from any experience ; it must contain nothing but *a priori* laws, which are necessary, and apply to the understanding universally.

Some logicians, indeed, presuppose in Logic *psychological* principles. But it is just as inappropriate to bring principles of this kind into Logic as to derive the science of morals from life. If we were to take the principles from psychology, that is, from observations on our understanding, we should merely see *how* thought takes place, and *how* it is affected by the manifold subjective hindrances and conditions ; so that this would lead only to the knowledge of *contingent* laws. But in Logic the question is not of *contingent*, but of *necessary* laws ; not how we do think, but how we ought to think. [173] The rules of Logic, then, must not be derived from the *contingent*, but from the *necessary* use of the understanding, which, without any psychology, a man finds in himself. In Logic we do not want to know how the understanding is and thinks, and how it has hitherto proceeded in thinking, but how it ought to proceed in thinking. Its business is to teach us the correct use of reason, that is, the use which is consistent with itself.

From the definition we have given of Logic, the other essential properties of this science may be deduced; namely—

4. That both as to its form and its *matter*, it is a rational science ; since its rules are not derived from experience, and since, at the same time, it has reason as its object. Logic, therefore, is a self cognition of the understanding and the reason, *not*, however, as to their power in respect of objects, but simply as to form. In Logic I do not ask *what* the understanding knows, and *how much* it can know, or *how far* its knowledge reaches ; for that would be self cognition in respect of its *material* use, and therefore belongs to metaphysics. In Logic, the question is only : *How will the understanding know itself ?*

5. Finally, being a science which is rational both in form and matter, Logic is a *Doctrine*, or *demonstrated theory*. For as it does not concern itself with the common and merely empirical use of the understanding and the reason, but solely with the universal and necessary laws of thought, therefore it rests on *à priori* principles, from which all its rules can be derived and proved, as rules to which all rational knowledge must conform.

[174] By this character Logic is essentially distinguished from *Aesthetics*, which being a mere *criticism* of *Taste*, has no canon (law), but only *Form* (pattern or measure by which to judge), which consists in general agreement of opinion. Aesthetics, in fact, contains the rules of the agreement of knowledge with the laws of the sensibility ; Logic, on the contrary, contains the rules of the agreement of knowledge with the laws of the understanding and the reason. The former have only empirical principles, and therefore can never be a science or doctrine, if we mean by doctrine a dogmatic instruction founded on *à priori* principles, in which we discern everything by the understanding, without any information obtained from experience, and which gives us rules by following which the desired completeness is secured. Many persons, especially orators and poets, have attempted to reduce taste to a rational system, but they have never been able to arrive at a decisive judgment upon it. The philosopher Baumgarten, in Frankfort, had constructed the plan of an Aesthetic regarded as a science. But Home[1] has more correctly called Aesthetics Criticism, because it does not, like Logic, furnish *à priori* rules, which are adequate to determine the judgment, but procures its rules *à posteriori*, and merely generalises by comparison the empirical laws by which we take knowledge of the more perfect (beautiful) and the more imperfect.

Logic, therefore, is more than mere criticism ; it is a Canon which afterwards serves for the purpose of criticism, that is, serves as the principle by which to judge of every use of the understanding ; although only as to its correctness in respect of form, since it is not an organon any more than universal grammar is such.

On the other side, general logic being a propædeutic of every use of the understanding, is distinguished from *Transcendental* Logic, in which the object itself is conceived as an object of the understanding alone ; whereas general Logic applies to all objects universally.

---

[1] [Lord Kames, author of " Principles of Criticism."]

[175] Now, if we collect together all the essential attributes which belong to the complete determination of the conception of Logic, we must exhibit the following definition of it:

Logic is a Rational Science, both as to its form, and also its matter; an *à priori* science of the necessary laws of thought, not, however, in respect to any particular objects, but to all objects generally : accordingly it is a science of the right use of the understanding and the reason generally, not subjectively, that is, not according to empirical (psychological) principles as to how the understanding actually thinks, but objectively, that is, according to *à priori* principles, as to how it ought to think.

II.

CHIEF DIVISIONS OF LOGIC—TREATMENT—USE OF THIS SCIENCE— SKETCH OF A HISTORY OF LOGIC.

Logic is divided—

1. into *Analytic* and *Dialectic.*

Analytic discovers, by means of analysis, all the actions of reason which we exercise in thought. It is therefore an analytic of the Form of the Understanding and of the Reason, and is justly called the Logic of Truth, since it contains the necessary rules of all (formal) truth, without which truth our knowledge is untrue in itself, even apart from its objects. [176] It is therefore nothing more than a Canon for deciding on the formal correctness of our knowledge.

Should we desire to use this merely theoretical and general doctrine as a practical art, that is, as an Organon, it would become a *Dialectic :* a *logic of semblance (ars sophistica disputatoria)*, arising out of an abuse of the Analytic. inasmuch as by the *mere logical form* there is contrived the semblance of a true knowledge, the characters of which must, on the contrary, be derived from agreement with objects, and therefore from the *content*.

In former times dialectic was studied with great diligence. This art presented false principles in the semblance of truth, and sought, in accordance with these, to maintain things in semblance. Amongst the Greeks the dialecticians were advocates and rhetoricians who could lead the populace wherever they chose, because the populace lets itself be deluded with semblance. Dialectic was therefore at that time the art of semblance. In Logic, also, it was for a long time treated of under the name of the *Art of Disputation*, and for so long all logic and philosophy was the cultivation by certain chatter-heads of the art of semblance. But nothing can be more unworthy of a philosopher than the cultivation of such an art. It must therefore be altogether dropped in this aspect of it, and instead of it there must be introduced into Logic a critical examination of this semblance.

We should therefore have two parts of Logic; the *Analytic*, which should treat of the formal criteria of truth, and the *Dialectic*, which should contain the marks and rules by which we should be able to know that something does not agree with the formal criteria of truth, although it seems to agree with them. Dialectic in this aspect would have its use as a *Cathartic* of the understanding.

[177] It is customary to divide Logic further—

2. into *natural* or *popular*, and *artificial* or *scientific* Logic (*logica naturalis; logica scholastica s. artificialis*).

But this division is untenable. For natural Logic, or Logic of the pure reason (*sensus communis*), is properly not Logic, but an anthropological science which has only empirical principles, since it treats of the rules of the natural use of the understanding and the reason, which can only be known *in concreto*, and without our being conscious of them *in abstracto*.

3. A further division of Logic is into *theoretical* and *practical* Logic. But this division also is unsound.

General Logic, which being a mere canon, abstracts from all objects, cannot have any practical part. This would be a *contradictio in adjecto*, since a practical logic presupposes the knowledge of a certain kind of objects to which it is applied. We may therefore call every science a *practical logic ;* for in every-one we must have a form of thought. General Logic, therefore, considered as practical, can be nothing more than an *instruction in the technicalities of Learning in general*—an *Organon of the Scholastic Method*.

According to this division, then, Logic would have a *dogmatic* and a *technical* part. [178] The former might be called *Stoicheiology*, the latter *Methodology*. The practical or technical part of Logic would be a logical art in respect of arrangement, and of logical technical expressions and distinctions, serving to facilitate the action of the understanding.

In both parts, however, the technical as well as the dogmatical, there must not be the least regard paid either to objects or to the subject of thought. In the latter respect Logic might be divided—

4. into *Pure* and *Applied* Logic.

In Pure Logic we separate the understanding from the other mental faculties, and consider what it does alone and of itself. Applied Logic considers the understanding so far as it is combined with the other mental faculties, which influence its actions, and give it a perverse direction, so that it does not proceed according to the laws which itself perceives to be the right ones. Applied Logic ought properly not to be called Logic. It is a Psychology in which we consider what is the usual process in our thought, not what is the right one. It may, indeed, after all, tell us what we ought to do in order to make a right use of the understanding, under the manifold subjective hindrances and limitations. We may also learn from it what assists the right use of the understanding, its resources, or the means of remedying logical faults and errors. It is not, however, a propædeutic. For Psychology, out of which everything in Applied Logic must be taken, is a part of the philosophical sciences to which Logic is to be the propædeutic.

It is indeed said that Technic, or the method of constructing a science, ought to be treated of in the Applied Logic. [179] But this is useless, nay, even mischievous. One would thus begin to build before he has the materials; and provide the form where there is no content. In each science its own technic must be treated.

Lastly, as to what concerns—

5. the division of Logic into the logic of common *sense*, and that of the *speculative* understanding, we observe that this science cannot be so divided at all.

It cannot be a science of the speculative understanding. For if it were a logic of speculative knowledge or of the speculative use of reason, it would be an organon of other sciences, and not a mere propædeutic, applying to every possible use of understanding and reason.

Just as little can Logic be a product of common sense. Common sense is the faculty of discerning the rules of cognition *in concreto*. But Logic is a science of the rules of thought *in abstracto*.

We may, however, take the common understanding as the object of logic, and so far as this is the case, it will abstract from the special rules of the speculative understanding, and therefore will be distinguished from the Logic of the speculative understanding.

As regards the *treatment* of Logic, this may be either *scholastic* or *popular*.

It is *scholastic* when it is adapted to the desire of knowledge, to the capabilities and the cultivation of those who desire to treat the knowledge of logical rules as a science. It is *popular*, when it condescends to the capabilities and wants of those who do not wish to study Logic as a science, but only to use it to clear their understanding. [180] In the scholastic treatment the rules must be presented *in their generality*, or *in abstracto;* in the popular treatment, on the contrary, *in particular* or *in concreto*. The scholastic treatment is the foundation of the popular, for he alone is able to treat anything in a popular manner who could also treat it more thoroughly.

Moreover, we distinguish *treatment* from *method*. By *method* is to be understood the manner in which a certain object is to be thoroughly known. It must be derived from the nature of the science itself, and accordingly being a necessary order of thought determined thereby, it cannot be altered. *Treatment* signifies only the manner of communicating one's thoughts to others, in order to make a doctrine intelligible.

From what we have now said respecting the nature and object of Logic, we may form an estimate of the value of this science, and the utility of the study of it by a correct and definite standard.

Logic, then, is not a general Art of Discovery, nor an Organon of Truth ; it is not an Algebra, by help of which hidden truths may be discovered.

Nevertheless, it is useful and indispensable as a *criticism of knowledge ;* or for passing judgment on the common, as well as the speculative reason, not for the purpose of teaching it, but in order to make it *correct* and consistent with itself. For the logical principle of truth is consistency of the understanding with its own laws.

[181] Finally, as regards the history of Logic, we will only mention the following :—

Logic, as we have it, is derived from Aristotle's *Analytic*. This philosopher may be regarded as the father of Logic. He treated it as an Organon, and divided it into *Analytic* and *Dialectic*. His treatment is very scholastic, and is directed to the development of the most general and fundamental notions of logic. Of this, however, we can make no use, since almost everything ends in mere subtilties, except that the names of several actions of the understanding are taken from it.

Since Aristotle's time Logic has not gained much in extent, as indeed its nature forbids that it should. But it may gain in respect of *accuracy, definiteness,* and *distinctness.* There are but few sciences that can come into a permanent state, which admits of no further alteration. To these belong Logic and Metaphysics. Aristotle has omitted no essential point of the understanding; we have only become more accurate, methodical, and orderly.

It was believed indeed that Lambert's *Organon* would much enlarge Logic. But it contains nothing additional except more subtile divisions, which, like all correct subtilties, no doubt sharpen the understanding, but are of no essential use.

Amongst more recent philosophers there are two who have brought general Logic into vogue, Leibnitz and Wolff.

Malebranche and Locke have not treated of Logic proper, although they treat of the extent of knowledge and of the origin of concepts.

The general Logic of Wolff is the best we possess. Some have combined it with the Aristotelian, as, for example, Reusch.

[182] Baumgarten, a man who has in this respect much merit, abridged Wolff's Logic, and Meyer then commented on Baumgarten.

To the later logicians belongs also Crusius, who however did not consider what the true character of Logic is. For his Logic contains metaphysical principles, and in this respect, therefore, transcends the limits of this science; besides, it sets forth a criterion of truth which can be no criterion, and in this way leaves free course to all sorts of vagaries.

In our own times there has been no famous logician, and indeed we do not require any new discoveries in Logic, since it contains merely the form of thought.

III.

CONCEPTION OF PHILOSOPHY IN GENERAL—PHILOSOPHY CON-
SIDERED ACCORDING TO THE SCHOLASTIC CONCEPTION AND
ACCORDING TO THE COSMICAL CONCEPTION—ESSENTIAL RE-
QUIREMENTS AND OBJECTS OF PHILOSOPHIZING—THE MOST
GENERAL AND HIGHEST PROBLEMS OF THIS SCIENCE.

It is sometimes difficult to define what is meant by a science.
But science gains in precision by the establishment of a definite
conception of it, and many errors from different sources are thus
avoided which otherwise slip in when we are unable to distinguish the science from the cognate sciences.

Before, however, we attempt to give a definition of philosophy, we must inquire into the character of different branches of
knowledge; and since philosophical knowledge belongs to the
class of rational knowledge, we must define what is to be understood by this latter.

[183] Rational knowledge is opposed to *historical* knowledge.
The former is knowledge from principles (*ex principiis*); the
latter is knowledge from data (*ex datis*). Knowledge, however,
may have originated from reason, and yet be historical; as for
example, when a mere littérateur learns the product of the reason
of others, then his knowledge of such rational products is merely
historical.

We may, in fact, distinguish different kinds of knowledge
as follows :—

1. According to their *objective* origin, that is, according to
the sources from which alone the knowledge can be drawn. In
this respect all knowledge is either *rational* or *empirical*;

2. According to their *subjective* origin, that is, according to
the manner in which the knowledge can be acquired by the
individual. From this last point of view knowledge is either
rational or *historical*, no matter how it has originated. Accordingly, it is possible for a thing to be *objectively* a piece of
rational knowledge, which *subjectively* is only historical.

In some branches of rational knowledge it is injurious to know them only historically; in others this is indifferent. For instance, the navigator knows the rules of navigation historically from his charts, and that is sufficient for him. But if the juris-consult possesses his knowledge of law only historically, he is completely unfitted to be a judge, and still more to be a legislator.

From the distinction stated between *objective* and *subjective* rational knowledge, it is now clear that one might in a certain respect learn philosophy without being able to philosophize. He then that desires to become, properly speaking, a philosopher, must exercise himself in making a free use of his reason, not a mere imitative and, so to speak, mechanical use.

[184] We have defined rational knowledge as knowledge from principles, and from this it follows that it must be *à priori*. Now there are two branches of knowledge which are both *à priori*, but yet have many important differences; namely, Mathematics and Philosophy.

It is common to assert that Mathematics and Philosophy are distinguished from one another by the nature of their *object;* the former treating of *Quantity*, the latter of *Quality*. All this is false. The distinction of these sciences cannot depend on the object; for philosophy applies to everything, and therefore also to *quanta*, and mathematics also applies in part to every-thing, inasmuch as everything has quantity. It is only the *different kind of the rational knowledge, or of the use of reason* in mathematics and philosophy that constitutes the specific differ-ence between these two sciences. Philosophy is *Rational know-ledge from mere concepts;* Mathematics, on the contrary, is *Ra-tional knowledge from the construction of concepts*.

We *construct* concepts when we present them in intuition *à priori*, without experience, or when we present in intuition the object which corresponds to our concept of it. The mathema-tician can never make use of his reason by way of mere concepts, nor can the philosopher make use of his by construction of con-cepts. In mathematics we use Reason *in concreto;* the intuition, however, is not empirical, but we make something *à priori* the object of the intuition.

Herein, therefore, as we see, mathematics has an advantage over philosophy, in that the knowledge of the former is intuitive; that of the latter, on the contrary, only *discursive*. But the reason why we consider quantities more in mathematics lies in this [185], that magnitudes can be constructed *à priori* in intuition ; while qualities, on the contrary, cannot be presented in intuition.

Philosophy, then, is the system of philosophical cognitions, or of rational knowledge from concepts. This is the *scholastic conception* of this science. According to the *cosmic conception*[1] of it, it is the science of the ultimate ends of human reason. This high conception gives *dignity* to philosophy, that is, an absolute value. And it is this alone which has *intrinsic* value, and which first gives value to all other branches of knowledge.

The question is always asked in the end, What is the use of philosophizing, and of its final aim, Philosophy itself, as a science, considered according to the scholastic conception of it ?

In this scholastic signification of the word, philosophy aims only at *skill ;* in reference to the higher or cosmic conception, on the contrary, it aims at *utility*. In the former aspect, therefore, it is a doctrine of skill ; in the latter, a doctrine of wisdom ; it is the lawgiver of reason ; and hence the philosopher is *not* a *master of the art of reason*, but a *lawgiver*.

The master of the art of reason, or as Socrates calls him, the *philodoxus*,[2] strives merely for speculative knowledge, without concerning himself how much this knowledge contributes to the ultimate end of human reason : he gives rules for the use of reason for all kinds of ends. The practical philosopher, the teacher of wisdom by doctrine and example, is the true philo-

---

[1] ["Weltbegriff," 'relating to what must concern everyone.' Kr. d. r. V. p. 840, note.]

[2] [Plato, *Rep.* 480. The φιλόδοξος is the man who loves and contemplates πολλὰ καλά, πολλὰ δίκαια, but not αὐτὸ τὸ καλόν, αὐτὸ τὸ δίκαιον, as the φιλόσοφος. The former are objects of δόξα, opinion, not of true knowledge.]

sopher. For philosophy is the Ideal of a perfect wisdom, which shows us the ultimate ends of all human reason.

[186] Philosophy, in the scholastic conception of it, includes two parts :—First, a sufficient stock of rational knowledge ; and secondly, a systematic connexion of the parts of this knowledge, or a combination of them into the idea of a whole.

Not only does philosophy admit such a strictly systematic connexion, but it is the only science which in the most proper sense has a systematic connexion, and gives systematic unity to all other sciences.

But as to philosophy, in the cosmic conception of it (*in sensu cosmico*), this also may be called *a science of the highest maxims of the use of our reason* ; understanding by maxims the internal principle of choice amongst diverse ends.

For philosophy, in the latter sense, is the science of the relation of all knowledge and every use of reason to the ultimate end of human reason, to which, as supreme, all other ends are subordinated, and must be combined into unity in it.

The field of philosophy, in this sense, may be reduced to the following questions :—

1. What can I know ?
2. What ought I to do ?
3. What may I hope ?
4. What is Man ?

The first question is answered by *Metaphysics*, the second by *Morals*, the third by *Religion*, and the fourth by *Anthropology*. In reality, however, all these might be reckoned under anthropology, since the first three questions refer to the last.

The philosopher, therefore, must be able to determine—

1. The sources of human knowledge. [187]
2. The extent of the possible and useful employment of knowledge ; and lastly—
3. The limits of reason.

The last is the most useful, but also the most difficult, and is one about which the philodoxus does not concern himself.

Two things, chiefly, are required in a philosopher—1. Cultivation of talents and of skill, so as to use them for various ends. 2. Readiness in the use of all means to any ends that may be chosen. Both must be united ; for without knowledge one can never become a philosopher; yet never will knowledge alone constitute a philosopher, unless there is added a fitting combination of all his knowledge and skill into unity, and an insight into the harmony of the same with the highest ends of human reason.

No one can call himself a philosopher who cannot philosophize. Now, it is only by practice and independent use of one's reason that one can learn to philosophize.

How, indeed, can Philosophy be learned ? Every philosophical thinker builds his own work on the ruins, so to speak, of another; but nothing has ever been built that could be permanent in all its parts. It is, therefore, impossible to learn philosophy, even for this reason, that it *does not yet exist*. But even supposing that there were a philosophy *actually existing*, yet no one who learned it could say of himself that he was a philosopher, for his knowledge of it would still be only *subjectively historical*.

In Mathematics it is otherwise. This science may, to a certain extent, be learned ; for the proofs in it are so plain that everyone can be convinced of them ; [188] and besides, on account of its plainness, it can be, as it were, kept as a *certain* and *permanent* doctrine.

He who desires to learn to philosophize must, on the contrary, regard all systems of philosophy only as a *history of the use of reason*, and as objects for the exercise of his philosophical ability.

The true philosopher, therefore, must, as an independent thinker, make a free and independent, not a slavishly imitative, use of his reason. Nor must it be dialectical, that is, a use which aims only at giving to his knowledge an *appearance of truth* and *wisdom*. This is the business of the mere Sophist ; but thoroughly inconsistent with the dignity of the philosopher, as one who knows and teaches Wisdom.

For science possesses an intrinsic real value only as it is an

Organ of Wisdom. But as such, it is indispensable to Wisdom, so that one might well assert that Wisdom, without Science, is a mere shadow outline of a perfection to which we shall never attain.

He that hates science, and so much the more loves wisdom, is called a *Misologist*. Misology arises usually from a lack of scientific knowledge, and a certain kind of vanity combined therewith. Sometimes, however, persons fall into the error of misology who, at first, pursued the sciences with great diligence and success, but at last found in all their knowledge no satisfaction.

Philosophy is the only science which can procure for us this internal satisfaction, for it closes, as it were, the scientific circle, and thus by it first the sciences acquire order and connexion.

We must, therefore, for the sake of exercise in independent thought or philosophizing, look more to the *method* of employment of reason than to the propositions themselves, at which we have arrived by its means.

---

[189] IV.

SHORT SKETCH OF A HISTORY OF PHILOSOPHY.

There is some difficulty in defining the limits where the *common* use of reason ends and the *speculative* begins ; or where common rational knowledge becomes philosophy.

However, there is here a tolerably certain mark of distinction, namely the following :—

The knowledge of the universal *in abstracto* is *speculative* knowledge ; the knowledge of the universal *in concreto* is *common* knowledge. Philosophical knowledge is speculative knowledge of reason, and accordingly it begins there where the common use of reason begins to make attempts in the knowledge of the universal *in abstracto*.

From this account of the distinction between the common

and the speculative use of reason, we may judge from what nation the beginning of philosophy is to be dated. Amongst all nations the Greeks have been the first to philosophize, for they first attempted to cultivate rational knowledge, not with the help of figures, but *in abstracto ;* whereas all other nations attempted to make concepts intelligible only by images. So even at the present day there are nations, such as the Chinese and some Indians, who treat, indeed, of things which are taken from reason only, as of God, the immortality of the soul, and many such things, and who yet do not attempt to study the nature of these objects by concepts and rules *in abstracto.* They make here no separation between the use of reason *in concreto* and that *in abstracto.* [190] Amongst the Persians and Arabians there is, indeed, some speculative use of reason ; but they have borrowed the rules of this from Aristotle, and thus still from the Greeks. In the Zend Avesta of Zoroaster we do not discover the smallest trace of philosophy. And the same holds good of the highly-praised wisdom of the Egyptians, which, in comparison with Greek philosophy, was a mere child's play.

As in philosophy, so also in mathematics, the Greeks were the first who cultivated this branch of rational knowledge, inasmuch as they demonstrated every theorem from elementary principles.

When and *where,* however, amongst the Greeks the philosophical spirit first arose, this cannot be exactly defined. The first who introduced the use of the speculative reason, and to whom were attributed the first steps of human understanding to scientific culture is Thales, the founder of the Ionic sect. He bore the surname Natural Philosopher (φυσικός), although he was also a mathematician ; as indeed mathematics has always preceded philosophy.

The first philosophers clothed everything in figures. For poetry, which is nothing but a clothing of thoughts in figures, is older than prose. At first, therefore, men were obliged, even in the case of things which are simply objects of pure reason, to make use of figurative language and the poetical style. Pherecydes is said to have been the first prose writer.

After the Ionians came the Eleatics. The fundamental principle of the Eleatic philosophy, and its founder Xenophanes, was : In the senses is delusion and appearance ; in the understanding alone lies the source of truth.

[191] Amongst the philosophers of this school Zeno was distinguished as a man of great intellect and acuteness, and as a subtle dialectician.

Dialectic at first meant the art of the pure use of the understanding with reference to abstract concepts, separated from everything sensible. Hence the many eulogies of this art amongst the ancients. Afterwards, when those philosophers who altogether rejected the evidence of the senses were necessarily led by this doctrine into many subtilties, dialectic was degraded into the art of defending and of opposing every statement. And thus it became a mere exercise for the Sophists, who professed to discuss everything, and set themselves to give to illusion the aspect of truth, and to make black white. On this account also the name *Sophist*, which was once applied to the man who could discourse rationally and acutely about everything, now became so hateful and contemptible, and instead of it the name *Philosopher* was introduced.

About the time of the Ionic school there arose in Magna Græcia a man of rare genius, who not only also established a school, but also sketched and carried out a project, the like of which had never been. This man was Pythagoras, born at Samos. He founded a society of philosophers, who were united in a league by the law of silence. He divided his disciples into two classes ; that of the Acusmatics (ἀκουσματικοί), who were only allowed to hear, and that of the Acroamatics (ἀκροαματικοί), who were also allowed to ask questions.

[192] Some of his doctrines were *exoteric*, which he communicated to the whole people ; the rest were secret and *esoteric*, intended only for the members of his society, some of whom he took into his most intimate friendship, and separated entirely from the others. He made Physics and Theology, that is, the doctrine of the visible and of the invisible, the *vehicle* of his secret

doctrines. He also had various *symbols*, which perhaps were nothing but certain signs which the Pythagoreans used for the purpose of mutual understanding.

The object of his society seems to have been nothing else than : to purify religion from the popular delusions, to moderate tyranny, and to introduce into states a more constitutional system of government. This league, however, which the tyrants began to fear, was destroyed shortly before the death of Pythagoras, and this philosophical society was brought to an end, partly by persecution to death, and partly by the flight and banishment of the greatest part of its members. The few who remained were *novices*. And as these did not know much of the peculiar doctrines of Pythagoras, we cannot say anything certain and definite about their doctrines. Subsequently many doctrines were ascribed to him which were certainly fictitious. It is to be noted that Pythagoras was also a man of great mathematical ability.

The most important epoch of Greek philosophy begins with Socrates. For it was he who gave an entirely new *practical* direction to the philosophical spirit, and to all speculative minds. Moreover, he stands almost alone amongst men as the one whose conduct comes nearest to the Idea of a Wise Man.

Amongst his disciples the most famous is Plato, who employed himself more with the practical doctrines of Socrates ; [193] and amongst the disciples of Plato, Aristotle, who again raised speculative philosophy to a higher pitch.

Plato and Aristotle were succeeded by the Epicureans and the Stoics, which two sects were the most declared enemies of each other. The former placed the summum bonum in a *cheerful heart*, which they called *pleasure ;* the latter found it solely in the *elevation* and *strength of soul*, which enables a man to dispense with everything agreeable in life.

In speculative philosophy the Stoics were *dialectical*, in moral philosophy *dogmatical*, and they showed uncommon dignity in their practical principles, by which they scattered the seeds of the loftiest sentiments that ever existed. The founder of the

Stoic school was Zeno of Citium. The most famous Greek philosophers of this school were Cleanthes and Chrysippus.

The Epicurean school was never able to attain the same reputation as the Stoic. But whatever may be said of the Epicureans, this much is certain, they showed the greatest moderation in enjoyment of pleasure, and were the *best natural philosophers* amongst all the thinkers of Greece.

We may notice, further, that the principal Greek schools had special names. Thus, the school of Plato was called the *Academy;* that of Aristotle *Lyceum;* the school of the Stoics the *Porch* (στοά), a covered walk, from which the name Stoic was derived; the school of Epicurus *Gardens,* because Epicurus taught in gardens.

Plato's Academy was succeeded by three other academies, which were founded by his disciples. The first was founded by Speusippus, the second by Arcesilaus, and the third by Carneades.

These academies inclined to scepticism. The tone of thought in both Speusippus and Arcesilaus was sceptical, [194] and Carneades went still further in this direction. On this account the sceptics, those subtile, dialectical philosophers, were also called Academics. Accordingly, the Academics followed the first great doubter Pyrrho and his successors. Their teacher Plato had himself given occasion to this, inasmuch as he treated many of his doctrines in the form of *dialogue,* so that reasons *pro* and *contra* were adduced without his giving a decision on them himself, although he was himself very dogmatical.

If we take the epoch of scepticism as beginning with Pyrrho, we find a whole school of sceptics who were essentially distinguished from the dogmatical philosophers in their mode of thought and their philosophical method; inasmuch as they adopted as the first maxim of all philosophical reasoning, this— *to reserve one's judgment even where there is the greatest appearance of truth;* and propounded the principle that *philosophy consists in an equilibrium of judgment, and teaches us to detect false appearance.* Of these sceptics, however, nothing remains to us except the two works of Sextus Empiricus, in which he has collected all doubts.

When in the sequel philosophy passed from the Greeks to the Romans, it was not extended, for the Romans always remained only disciples.

Cicero was in speculative philosophy a disciple of Plato ; in morals he was a Stoic. The most celebrated followers of the Stoic sect were Epictetus, Antoninus, and Seneca. There were no *natural philosophers* among the Romans except Pliny the Elder, who has left a Natural History.

At last, culture disappeared amongst the Romans also, and Barbarism arose, until the Arabians, in the sixth and seventh centuries, began [195] to apply themselves to science, and to bring Aristotle into repute again. Now the sciences again sprang up in the West, and especially the reputation of Aristotle, who was followed, however, in a slavish manner. In the eleventh and twelfth centuries the Schoolmen came forward ; they *explained* Aristotle, and pushed his subtilties to an unlimited extent. Men employed themselves with nothing but abstractions. This scholastic method of bastard philosophizing was suppressed at the time of the Reformation ; and now there were Eclectics in philosophy, that is, independent thinkers, who attached themselves to no school, but sought and accepted the truth wherever they found it.

For the improvement of philosophy in modern times we have to thank *partly* the greater study of nature, *partly* the combination of mathematics with natural philosophy. The study of these sciences introduced order in thought, and this extended itself also to the special branches and departments of philosophy proper. The first and greatest student of nature of the modern period was Bacon of Verulam. He trod in his inquiries the path of experience, and directed attention to the importance and necessity of *observation* and *experiment* for the discovery of truth. It is hard, however, to say what is properly the source of the improvement of speculative philosophy. Descartes has no small merit in this respect, inasmuch as he largely contributed to give *distinctness to thought* by means of the criterion of truth which he propounded, and which he placed in the *clearness and evidence of the cognition.*

Amongst the greatest and most meritorious reformers of philosophy in our times are to be reckoned Leibnitz and Locke. The latter endeavoured to analyse the human understanding, and to show what faculties and what operations thereof belonged to this or that part of knowledge. [196] He did not, however, complete his investigation; moreover, his procedure is dogmatic, although his labours had the useful result that men began to study the nature of the soul better and more thoroughly.

The special dogmatic method of philosophizing, proper to Leibnitz and Wolff, was very faulty. Moreover, there is in it so much that is delusive, that it is necessary to suspend the whole process, and instead of it to introduce the Method of the Critical Philosophy; which consists in investigating the procedure of the reason itself, analysing the whole human faculty of knowledge, and trying how far its *limits* extend.

In our age Natural Philosophy is in the most flourishing condition, and amongst the students of nature there are some great names, for example, Newton. More recent philosophers cannot properly be named at present, as of distinguished and lasting fame, since everything is, as it were, in a floating condition. What one builds, the next pulls down.

In moral philosophy we have not advanced beyond the Ancients. But as to metaphysics, it seems as if we had lost heart in the investigation of metaphysical truths. There is displayed at the present time a sort of indifferentism towards this science, so that persons seem to plume themselves on speaking as contemptuously of metaphysical inquiries into nature as if they were mere grubbing. And yet metaphysics is the genuine, true philosophy.

Our age is the age of criticism, and it is necessary to see what will come of the critical attempts of our time in reference to philosophy, and metaphysics in particular.

KNOWLEDGE IN GENERAL—INTUITIVE AND DISCURSIVE KNOW-
LEDGE — INTUITION AND CONCEPT, AND THE DISTINCTION
BETWEEN THEM — LOGICAL AND AESTHETICAL PERFECTION
OF KNOWLEDGE.

All our knowledge has a twofold relation : *first*, a relation to
the Object ; *secondly*, a relation to the Subject. In the former
respect it is related to the idea presented [Vorstellung] ; in the
second to consciousness, the general condition of all knowledge.
(Consciousness is the idea that another idea is in me).

In every act of knowledge we must distinguish the Matter,
that is, the Object, and the Form, that is, the manner in which
we take knowledge of the object. If a savage, for example, sees
a house in the distance, the use of which he does not know, he
has, no doubt, the same object presented to him as another man
who knows it definitely as a habitation intended for men. But
the form of this knowledge of the same object is different in the
two men. In the one it is mere Intuition ; in the other it is
Intuition and Concept combined.

The diversity of the form of knowledge rests on a condition
that accompanies every act of knowledge, namely, consciousness. Am I conscious of the idea, it is *clear;* am I not conscious of it, it is *obscure.*

As consciousness is the essential condition of every logical
form of knowledge, Logic can and must concern itself only with
clear, not at all with obscure, ideas. In logic we do not see how
ideas originate, but simply how they agree with the logical
form. [198] Logic cannot treat at all of mere ideas, and their
possibility. That it leaves to Metaphysics. It concerns itself
only with the rules of thought in Concepts, Judgments, and Inferences, it being by means of these that all thought takes place.
No doubt something precedes before an idea becomes a concept.
This we shall show in its proper place. Here, however, we do
not inquire how ideas originate. Logic, indeed, treats also of

the act of knowing, because in the act of knowing there is already Thought. But an idea is not yet knowledge; but knowledge always presupposes the presence of the idea. And this latter can by no means be explained. For we could not explain *what an idea is*, except by means of another idea.

All clear ideas being those to which alone logical rules can be applied, may be distinguished into *Distinct* and *Indistinct*. If we are conscious of the whole idea, but not of the plurality contained in it, then the idea is indistinct. An illustration may serve to explain this.

We see in the distance a country-house. If we are conscious that the object perceived is a house, we must necessarily have also an idea of the different parts of this house; the windows, doors, &c. For if we did not see the parts we should not see the house itself. But we are not conscious of this idea of the plurality of its parts, and hence our idea of the object thought of is itself an indistinct idea.

As an example of indistinctness in concepts, we may take the concept of Beauty. Every one has a clear concept of beauty. But this concept contains several attributes; amongst others, that the beautiful must be something [199] that—1° strikes the senses, and—2° generally pleases. Now, if we cannot state in detail to ourselves these and other attributes of the beautiful, our concept of it is indistinct.

Indistinct ideas are called by the disciples of Wolff *confused*. But this expression is unsuitable, since the opposite of confusion is not distinctness, but order. It is true, distinctness is an effect of order, and indistinctness an effect of disorder, and therefore every confused cognition is also indistinct. But the converse does not hold; not every indistinct cognition is confused. For in cognitions which do not involve any plurality there is no order, and no confusion.

This is the case with all *simple* ideas which are never distinct; not because there is confusion in them, but because there is no plurality. These, therefore, must be called indistinct, but not confused.

Even in complex ideas, in which a plurality of attributes may

be distinguished, the indistinctness is often the result not of confusion, but of *weakness of consciousness*. Thus, something may
be distinct as to its *form*, that is, I may be conscious of the plurality in the idea, but as to its *matter* the distinctness may be
less if the degree of consciousness is less, although there is no
lack of order. This is the case with abstract ideas.

Distinctness itself may be twofold :—

First, *sensible distinctness*. This consists in the consciousness
of the manifold in intuition. For instance, I see the Milky
Way as a white stripe ; the rays of light from the individual
stars in it must necessarily have reached my eye. [200] But
the idea of it was only clear, and becomes distinct only when
the telescope is applied, because now I discern the individual
stars contained in it.

Secondly, *intellectual distinctness ; distinctness in concepts*, or
distinctness to the understanding. This depends on analysis of
the concept in reference to the plurality contained in it. For
instance, in the concept of Virtue there are contained as attributes—1° the concept of freedom ; 2° the concept of obedience
to rules (duty) ; 3° the concept of the subjugation of the power
of the inclinations, in so far as they conflict with these rules.
When we *thus* analyse the concept of virtue into its separate
constituents, we make it distinct to ourselves. We do not hereby
add anything to a concept, we only define it. Hence, distinctness is an improvement of concepts, not as to their *matter*, but
as to their *form* only.

When we reflect on our cognitions in reference to the two
essentially distinct faculties of sensibility and understanding
from which they arise, we come upon the distinction between
intuitions and concepts. All our cognitions, considered in this
respect, are either *intuitions* or *concepts*. The former have their
source in the sensibility—the faculty of intuitions ; the latter in
the understanding—the faculty of concepts. This is the *logical*
distinction between the understanding and the sensibility, according to which the latter gives only intuitions, the former
only concepts. Both faculties may certainly be considered in

another aspect also, and defined in a different manner ; namely, the sensibility as the faculty of *receptivity*, the understanding as a faculty of *spontaneity*. But this mode of definition is not logical but *metaphysical*. [201] It is usual also to call the sensibility the *lower*, and the understanding the *higher*, faculty ; for this reason that the sensibility only supplies the mere material for thought, while the understanding deals with this material, and brings it under rules or concepts.

On the distinction here stated between *intuitive* and *discursive* cognitions, or between intuitions and concepts, is founded the difference of the *aesthetical* and the *logical* perfection of cognition.

A cognition may be perfect, either according to laws of the sensibility, or according to laws of the understanding ; in the former case it is *aesthetically* perfect, in the latter *logically* perfect. These two kinds of perfection, then, are distinct ; the former has reference to the sensibility, the latter to the understanding. The logical perfection of the cognition rests on its agreement with the object, and therefore on laws which are *universally valid*, and hence can be estimated by *à priori* standards. Aesthetical perfection consists in the agreement of the cognition with the subject, and is founded on the special sensibility of man. Hence, in aesthetical perfection there are no laws objectively and universally valid, in reference to which it could be estimated *à priori* in a manner valid for all thinking beings. Nevertheless, as there are also general laws of the sensibility, which although not holding good objectively, and for all thinking beings, yet are valid for the whole of humanity, hence, we may conceive an aesthetical perfection which contains the ground of a subjectively universal satisfaction. This is Beauty ; that which pleases the senses in intuition, and just for this reason may be the object of a universal satisfaction, since the laws of intuition are universal laws of sensibility.

[202] This agreement with the universal laws of sensibility makes a specific distinction between the *properly, independently Beautiful*, the essence of which consists in the mere *form*, and the *agreeable*, which merely pleases in sensation by stimulating

emotion, and for this reason can only be the ground of a mere personal satisfaction.

It is this essential aesthetical perfection, also, which of all others harmonises and combines best with logical perfection.

Considered in this aspect, then, aesthetical perfection in point of essential beauty may contribute to logical perfection. In another respect, however, it is even injurious to it, since in the case of aesthetical perfection we look only to the non-essential beauty—the attractive or moving—which pleases the senses in the mere sensation, and refers not to the mere form, but to the matter of the sensibility. For what stimulates and causes emotion can most easily spoil the logical perfection of our cognitions and judgments.

There always remains, indeed, a sort of conflict, which cannot be completely reconciled, between the aesthetical and the logical perfection of our knowledge. The understanding demands to be instructed, the sensibility to be quickened: the former desires insight, the latter easy grasp. If cognitions are to instruct, they must so far be thorough; if they are also to entertain, they must also be beautiful. If the treatment of a subject is beautiful, but shallow, it can only please the sensibility, not the understanding; if, on the contrary, it is thorough, but dry, then it may please the understanding, but not the sensibility.

[203] Since, however, it is required by human nature, and for the purpose of popularising the cognition, that we should try to unite both kinds of perfection, we must take care to give aesthetic perfection to those cognitions which are capable of it, and thus to give popularity to a cognition which is scholastic and logically perfect. In this endeavour we must not neglect the following rules, viz.—1°, That the logical perfection is the basis of all other perfections, and therefore must not be quite postponed or sacrificed to any other. 2°, That the *formal* aesthetical perfection be chiefly regarded; that is, the agreement of a cognition with the laws of intuition; since it is just in this that the essential beauty consists which can best be united with logical perfection. 3°, To be very sparing with

emotional excitement, by which a cognition works on feeling and contains an interest, for by this the attention is so easily drawn from the object to the subject, and it is obvious that there must arise from this a very mischievous influence upon the logical perfection of the cognition.

In order that the essential differences that exist between the logical and the aesthetical perfections may be made still clearer, not merely in general, but on several different sides, we will compare the two in reference to the four principal moments of Quantity, Quality, Relation, and Modality, with which the estimation of the perfection of cognition turns.

A cognition is perfect—1°, as to Quantity, when it is *universal;* 2°, as to Quality, when it is *distinct;* [204] 3°, as to Relation, when it is *true;* and lastly, 4°, as to Modality, when it is *certain.*

Considered from these points of view, then, a cognition will be logically perfect as to Quantity when it possesses objective universality (universality of the concept or of the rule) : as to Quality when it possesses objective distinctness (distinctness in the concept) : as to Relation when it possesses objective truth ; and lastly, as to Modality when it possesses objective certainty.

To these logical perfections correspond the following aesthetical perfections in reference to these four chief moments, viz. :—

1°. *Aesthetical Universality.*—This consists in the applicability of a cognition to a multitude of objects which serve as examples of its application, and by means of which also it becomes useful for the purpose of popularity.

2°. *Aesthetical Distinctness.*—This is distinctness in intuition, in which, by means of examples, a concept conceived abstractly is presented or explained *in concreto.*

3°. *Aesthetical Truth.*—A mere subjective truth, which consists only in the agreement of the cognition with the subject and the laws of sensible appearance, and consequently is nothing more than a universal semblance.

4°. *Aesthetical Certainty.*—This depends on what the testimony of the senses declares to be necessary, that is, what is established by sensation and experience.

[205] In the perfections just mentioned, there are always two elements which, by their harmonious union, produce perfection in general, viz., Plurality and Unity. In the understanding the unity lies in the concept ; in the sensibility in the intuition.

Mere plurality, without unity, cannot satisfy us. Hence, amongst all perfections, the chief is truth, because it is the ground of unity, by the reference of our cognition to an object. Even in aesthetical perfection, truth remains always the *conditio sine qua non*, the most important negative condition, without which a thing cannot please the taste generally. No one, therefore, may hope to succeed in polite literature, unless the foundation of his knowledge is laid in logical perfection. It is in the greatest possible combination of logical with aesthetical perfection with respect to such cognitions, as should both instruct and entertain, that the character and art of true genius are shown.

VI.

SPECIAL LOGICAL PERFECTIONS OF COGNITION.

A.—*Logical Perfection of Cognition as to Quantity—Quantity— Extensive and Intensive Quantity—Fulness and Thorough- ness ; or, Importance and Fruitfulness of the Cognition— Determination of the Horizon of our Knowledge.*

The Quantity of a cognition may be taken in a twofold sense, either as *extensive* or as *intensive*. [206] The former refers to the *extent* of the cognition, and accordingly consists in the number and variety of its contents, the latter refers to its intrinsic value, which concerns the logical importance and fruitfulness of a cognition considered as the ground of many and important consequences (*non multa sed multum*).

In enlarging our knowledge, or perfecting it in its extensive quantity, it is well to consider how far a cognition is consistent with our ends and our capacities. This consideration concerns the determination of the *horizon* of our knowledge, by which is to be understood the *due proportion of the sum total of the cognitions, to the capacities and ends of the subject.*

The horizon may be determined :—

1°. Logically, according to the cognitive faculties as far as *the understanding* is concerned. In this case we have to judge : how far we can go in our knowledge ; how far we must go in it, and how far certain cognitions serve, in a logical point of view, as means to this or that main branch of knowledge as our end.

2°. Aesthetically, according to Taste as far as *feeling* is concerned. The man who determines his horizon aesthetically, seeks to arrange the science according to the taste of the public, that is, to make it *popular*, or, generally speaking, to acquire only such knowledge as can be generally communicated, and in which the unlearned class take pleasure and interest.

3°. Practically, according to Utility as far as the *will* is concerned. The practical horizon, being determined according to the influence that a cognition has on our morality, is *pragmatical*, and of the greatest importance.

[207] Thus, the horizon concerns the estimation and determination of what a man *can* know, what he *may* know, and what he *ought* to know.

Now, as to the theoretically or logically determined horizon, with which alone we are now concerned, this may be considered either from the *objective* or the *subjective* point of view.

In reference to the *objects*, the horizon is either *historical* or *rational*. The former is much more extensive than the latter ; nay, it is immeasurably great, for our historical knowledge has no limits. The rational horizon, on the contrary, can be fixed ; we can determine, for instance, to what kind of objects mathematical knowledge cannot be extended. So also with respect to the philosophical rational knowledge, how far our reason can proceed *à priori* without any experience.

In reference to the subject, the horizon is either *universal* and *absolute*, or *particular* and *conditioned* (personal horizon).

By the former is to be understood the congruence of the limits of human knowledge with the limits of all human perfections in general.   Here then the question is : What can man, as man, know ?

The determination of the personal horizon depends on manifold empirical conditions, and special circumstances—as, for example, age, sex, position, way of life, and the like.   Thus, every particular class of men has its own particular horizon relative to its special powers of knowledge, its ends, and points of view ; every person, also, has his own horizon depending on the measure of his own individual powers, and his own point of view.   Lastly, we can also conceive a horizon of *sound sense,* and a horizon of *science,* [208] which latter requires principles in order to determine according to them *what we can know, and what we cannot know.*

What we *cannot* know is *above* our horizon.   What we dare not or need not know is *outside* our horizon.   This latter, however, can only hold good *relatively* in reference to this or that particular private end, to the attainment of which certain cognitions not only contribute nothing, but might be even a hindrance.   For there is no knowledge that is absolutely and in every respect useless, although we may not always be able to see the use of it.   It is, therefore, a foolish and unsound objection that is made by shallow minds to the great men who devote themselves with laborious diligence to scientific studies, when it is asked, *What is the use of that ?*   This question should never be asked with reference to a scientific inquiry.   Granted, that a science could only solve questions respecting some possible object, it would be quite useful enough.   Every logically perfect cognition has always some possible use which, although as yet unknown *to us,* may perhaps be discovered by posterity.   If, in the cultivation of the sciences, men had always looked to the material gain, the utility resulting, we should not possess either Arithmetic or

Geometry. Our understanding, moreover, is so constituted that it finds satisfaction in mere insight, and even more than in the resulting utility. This was remarked by Plato. Man feels in this his own excellence; he feels what it is to possess understanding. Men who do not feel this must envy the beasts. The *intrinsic* value which cognitions possess, by their logical perfection, is not to be compared with their *extrinsic* value or value in application.

[209] That which lies *outside* our horizon, as what for our purposes it is not necessary to know, must be understood *relatively*, not at all in an absolute sense ; and the same holds good of what lies *below* our horizon, and which, as being *injurious* for us, we *ought* not to know.

With respect to the enlargement and demarcation of our knowledge, the following rules are to be recommended :—

1°. To determine our horizon *early*, but yet not until we can determine it ourselves, which usually is not before the age of twenty.

2°. Not to change it easily and often (not to pass from one to another).

3°. Not to measure the horizon of others by our own, and not to regard that as useless which is not useful to *us ;* it would be unreasonable to wish to determine the horizon of others, since we do not sufficiently know either their capacities or their purposes.

4°. Neither to extend it too much, nor to limit it too much. For he who wants to know too much, in the end knows nothing ; and, on the other hand, he who thinks of some things that they do not concern him, often deceives himself ; as, for example, if the philosopher supposed that he could dispense with a knowledge of history.

5°. To determine previously the absolute horizon of the whole human race (in past and future times), and in particular

6°. To determine the place that our science takes in the horizon of all knowledge. [210] For this an Encyclopædia of

science is serviceable, as a kind of map of the world of the
sciences.

7°. In determining one's own horizon, to examine carefully
for what branch of knowledge one has the most ability and inclination ; what is more or less necessary in reference to certain
duties, what is not compatible with *necessary* duties.

Lastly, 8°. To try always rather to enlarge our horizon
than to narrow it.

There is no reason to apprehend from the enlargement of
knowledge that which D'Alembert fears from it; for we are
not oppressed by the burden, but cramped by the narrowness
of space for our knowledge. Critical study of the reason, of
history and historical books, a largeness of mind which goes
into human knowledge *en gros* and not merely *en détail*, will
constantly make the extent smaller without diminishing its
content. Only the dross will fall away from the metal, or the
baser vehicle the husk, which was so long necessary. With
the enlargement of Natural History, of Mathematics, &c.,
new methods will be discovered which will put our old knowledge in smaller compass, and enable us to dispense with the
multitude of books. On the discovery of such new methods and
principles it will depend that without burdening the memory
we can by their help find out everything ourselves as we wish.
Therefore he displays true genius with respect to history who
groups it under ideas which can endure.

[211] Opposed to the logical perfection of knowledge with
respect to its extent is ignorance, a *negative* imperfection, or imperfection of *want*, which on account of the limits of our understanding continues inseparable from our knowledge.

Ignorance may be considered from an objective or from a
subjective point of view.

1°. Objectively considered, ignorance is either material or
formal. The former consists in a lack of historical, the latter
in a lack of rational knowledge. One should not be absolutely

ignorant in any branch, but one may limit his historical knowledge in order to pay more attention to the rational, or *vice
versa*.

2°. Subjectively viewed, ignorance is either a learned *scientific* ignorance, or *common*. The man who distinctly sees the
limits of knowledge, and therefore the field of ignorance from
which it starts ; the philosopher, for instance, who perceives and
proves how little from want of the requisite data we can know
of the structure of gold, is ignorant by rule of art, or ignorant in
a learned manner. On the other hand, the man who is ignorant
without perceiving the reasons of the limits of ignorance, or
troubling himself about them, is ignorant in a common unsci-
entific manner. Such a man does not even know that he knows
nothing. For one can never be aware of his own ignorance except by means of science ; just as a blind man can form no conception of darkness until he has acquired sight.

Accordingly the knowledge of one's ignorance presupposes
science, and at the same time makes a man modest, whereas
imagined knowledge puffs up. So Socrates' want of knowledge
was a praiseworthy ignorance ; it was properly a knowledge of
his want of knowledge, as he himself confessed. Those persons
then who possess much knowledge, and with all that are amazed
at the amount of what they do not know, are not open to the
charge of ignorance.

[212] In general, ignorance of things, the knowledge of
which lies *above* our horizon, is *not blameable* (*inculpabilis*). Ignorance is also *allowable* (though only in a relative sense) in
respect to the speculative use of our faculties so far as the objects in this case lie *outside* although *not above* our horizon. But
ignorance is *shameful* in things which it is both necessary and
easy for us to know.

There is a difference between *not knowing* a thing, and *ig-
noring* it, that is, taking no notice of it. It is good to ignore
much which it is not good for us to know. Different from both
is *abstraction*. We abstract from a cognition when we ignore
its application, by which means we obtain it *in abstracto*, and

can then consider it better in general as a principle. Such an abstracting from that which in the cognition of a thing does not belong to our purpose is useful and praiseworthy.

Logicians are usually historically ignorant.

Historical knowledge without definite limits is the knowledge of a *polyhistor*. This puffs up. The term *polymathy* applies to rational knowledge [similarly unlimited]. Both historical and rational knowledge extended without definite limits may be called *pansophy*. To historical knowledge belongs the science of the instruments of learning—philology, which comprehends a critical knowledge of books and languages (literature and linguistic).

Mere polyhistory is a cyclopean learning which lacks one eye—the eye of philosophy; and a cyclops in mathematics, history, natural science, philology and languages, is a learned man who is great in all these branches, but thinks that all philosophy about them may be dispensed with.

[213] A part of philology consists in the *humanities* [or *literæ humaniores*], by which is understood the knowledge of the ancients, which promotes *the union of science with taste*, refines coarseness, and promotes the urbanity and ease of intercourse in which polite learning consists.

The *humaniora* (or polite letters) therefore are concerned with instruction in what subserves the cultivation of taste, according to the model of the ancients. To this belong, for example, eloquence, poetry, the being well read in the classical authors, &c. All these polite studies may be reckoned as belonging to the *practical* part of philology, which aims at the formation of taste. If, however, we make a distinction between the mere philologist and the humanist, or man of polite learning, the difference will be that the former seeks in the ancients the instruments of *learning*, the latter, on the other hand, the instruments of the *formation of taste*.

The student of *belles lettres*, or *bel esprit*, is a humanist who follows contemporary models in living languages. He is, therefore, not a learned man, for it is only *dead* languages that are at present learned languages, but a mere *dilettante* in matters

of taste in accordance with fashion, and has no need of the
ancients. We might call him the ape of the humanist. The
polyhistor must as a philologist be a *linguist* and *literary* man ;
and as a humanist he must be a classical scholar. As a philologist he is cultivated, as a humanist he is civilized.

With respect to the sciences, there are two ways in which
the prevailing taste may be corrupted, *pedantry* and *dilettantism*
[Galanterie]. The one pursues the sciences merely for the
school, and thereby limits them in respect of their *use ;* the
other pursues them merely for the sake of social intercourse,
and thereby limits them with respect to their *content*.

[214] The pedant may be regarded as the man of learning,
in contrast to the man of the world ; and so far he is the con-
ceited man of learning without knowledge of the world, that is,
without knowledge of the way to make his science a market-
able commodity, or he is to be regarded as the man of skill, but
only in *matters of form*, not as to essence and purpose. In the
latter signification he is a *formalist ;* knowing little of the
kernel of things, he looks only to the dress and the shell. He
is the caricature of the methodical man. We might therefore
call pedantry petty carefulness and useless exactness (micrology)
in matters of form. And such scholastic formality outside the
schools is to be met with not only in learned men and learned
matters, but also in other classes and in other things. The
ceremonial in courts, in social intercourse—what is it but a
pursuit of formalities? In the army it is not altogether so,
although it appears so. But in conversation, in dress, in diet,
in religion, much pedantry often prevails.

A fitting accuracy in matters of form is *thoroughness* (scholastic perfection). Pedantry, then, is an *affectation* of thoroughness, just as dilettantism, being a mere suitor for the applause
of fashion, is nothing but an *affectation* of popularity ; for it
only seeks to recommend itself to the reader, and therefore not
to offend him even by a single hard word.

To avoid pedantry, there is required not only an extensive
acquaintance with the sciences themselves, but also with the use

of them.   Hence it is that only the truly learned man can free
himself from pedantry, which is always the attribute of a shallow mind.

In endeavouring to give to our knowledge the perfection of
scholastic thoroughness, [215] and at the same time popularity,
without falling into these errors of affectation of thoroughness
or affectation of popularity, we must first of all look to the
scholastic perfection of our knowledge—the scholastic form of
thoroughness—and only after that study how to make this me-
thodically learned knowledge truly popular, that is, easy and
generally communicable to others, yet so that thoroughness is
not supplanted by popularity.   For we must not, for the sake
of popularity, that is, to please the public, sacrifice scholastic
perfection, without which all science is nothing but toying and
trifling.

Now in order to learn true popularity one should read
the ancients; for instance, Cicero's philosophical writings; the
poets, Horace, Virgil, &c. ; amongst the moderns, Hume,
Shaftesbury, and others.   Men who all have had much intercourse with cultured society, without which one cannot be
popular.   For true popularity requires much practical knowledge of the world and of men, knowledge of the notions, the
tastes, and the inclinations of men, to which one must constantly have regard in exposition, and even in the choice of
fitting expressions adapted to popularity.   Such a condescen-
sion to the comprehension of the public and to familiar expressions, while scholastic perfection is not neglected, but
only the clothing of one's thoughts is so contrived that the
scaffolding—what is *scholastic* and *technical* in that perfection—
is not allowed to be seen (just as a person draws lines with lead
pencil, on which he writes and which he then rubs out), this
truly popular perfection is in reality a great and rare perfection,
which gives evidence of much insight into science.   Besides
many other merits it has this, [216] that it may supply a test
for complete insight into a thing.   For the mere scholastic testing of knowledge still leaves room for the doubt whether the
examination is not one-sided, and whether the knowledge itself

has a value admitted by all men. The schools have their prejudices as well as common sense. One here improves the other.
It is therefore important to test a cognition with men whose
understanding is not dependent on any school.

This perfection of knowledge by which it is fitted for easy
and general communication, may be called the *external extension*,
or the extensive magnitude of a cognition, since it is extended
externally amongst many men.

As there are so many and varied branches of knowledge, it
is well to make a plan for ourselves according to which we may
arrange the sciences in the manner best adapted for our purposes. All departments of knowledge stand in a certain natural
relation to one another. Now if in endeavouring to enlarge our
knowledge we neglect this natural connexion, all our manifold
knowledge will result in nothing but mere *rhapsody*. But if
we make some one science our end, and consider all other parts
of knowledge only as means to it, then we impart to our knowledge a certain systematic character. And in order to be able
to proceed in the enlargement of our knowledge on such a well-
ordered and appropriate plan, we must try to discover that
mutual connexion of different branches of knowledge. In this
we are guided by the Architectonic of the sciences, which is a
system in which *the sciences are considered with respect to their
relationship and systematic combination into a whole comprising
the knowledge interesting humanity.*

[217] Now as to what concerns in particular the *intensive*
magnitude of knowledge, that is, its value or importance, which,
as above remarked, differs essentially from its extensive magnitude, its mere extent, we shall only make the following few
remarks :—

1°. A cognition that applies *to the whole* in the use of reason
is to be distinguished from *subtilty* in *petty matters* (micrology).

2°. Every cognition may be called *logically important* which
promotes logical perfection *as to form ;* for example, every mathematical theorem, every distinctly perceived law of nature,

every correct philosophical explanation. *Practical* importance cannot be *foreseen*, but must always be waited for.

3°. Importance must not be confounded with *difficulty*. A cognition may be difficult without being important, and *vice versa*. Difficulty, therefore, does not decide either for or against the value and importance of a cognition. This depends on the magnitude or the number of its consequences. The more or the greater consequences a cognition has, and the more use can be made of it, so much the more important it is. A knowledge without important consequences is called a mere subtilty. Such was, for instance, the scholastic philosophy.

---

[218] VII.

B.—*Logical Perfection of Knowledge as to Relation—Truth—Material and Logical or Formal Truth—Criteria of Logical Truth—Falsity and Error—Semblance as a source of Error—Means of avoiding Error.*

An important perfection of Knowledge, nay, the essential and inseparable condition of all its perfection, is Truth. Truth is said to consist in the agreement of knowledge with the object. According to this mere verbal definition, then, my knowledge, in order to be true, must agree with the object. Now, I can only compare the object with my knowledge by this means, namely, *by taking knowledge of it.* My knowledge, then, is to be verified by itself, which is far from being sufficient for truth. For as the object is external to me, and the knowledge is in me, I can only judge whether my knowledge of the object agrees with my knowledge of the object. Such a circle in explanation was called by the ancients *Diallelos*. And the logicians were accused of this fallacy by the sceptics, who remarked that this account of truth was as if a man before a judicial tribunal should make a statement, and appeal in support of it to a wit-

ness whom no one knows, but who defends his own credibility
by saying that the man who had called him as a witness is an
honourable man. The charge was certainly well-founded. *Only*
the solution of the problem referred to is absolutely impossible
for any man.

The question is in fact this : whether and how far there is
a certain, universal, and practically applicable criterion of truth.
For this is the meaning of the question, What is Truth ?

[219] In order to be able to decide this important question,
we must distinguish that in our knowledge which belongs to the
matter of it, and refers to the *object*, from that which concerns
the *mere form* as the condition without which knowledge would
not be knowledge at all. Attending then to this distinction
between the *objective* and *material* and the *subjective* and *formal*
aspect of our knowledge, the preceding question falls into these
two :—

1°. Is there a universal material criterion ? and
2°. Is there a universal formal criterion of truth ?

A universal material criterion of truth is not possible ; the
term is indeed self-contradictory. For being *universal* it would
necessarily abstract from all distinction of objects, and yet being
a material criterion, it must be concerned with just this distinction in order to be able to determine whether a cognition agrees
with the very object to which it refers, and not merely with some
object or other, which would really mean nothing. But material
truth must consist in this agreement of a cognition with the
definite object to which it refers. For a cognition which is
true in reference to one object, may be false in reference to
other objects. It is therefore absurd to demand a universal
material criterion of truth, which is at once to abstract and not
to abstract from all distinction of objects.

But if we ask for *a universal formal* criterion of truth, it is
very easy to decide that there may be such a criterion. For
formal truth consists simply in the agreement of the cognition
with itself when we abstract from all objects whatever, and
from every distinction of objects. [220] And hence the universal

formal criteria of truth are nothing but universal logical marks of agreement of cognitions with themselves, or, what is the same thing, with the general laws of the understanding and the reason.

These formal universal criteria are certainly not sufficient for objective truth, but yet they are to be viewed as its *conditio sine qua non.*

For before the question, whether the cognition agrees with the object must come the question, whether it agrees with itself (as to form). And this is the business of Logic.

The formal criteria of truth in Logic are—

1°. The Principle of Contradiction.
2°. The Principle of Sufficient Reason.

The first determines the *logical possibility*, the latter the *logical actuality* of a cognition.

In fact the logical truth of a cognition requires—

First, that it be logically possible, that is, be *not self-contradictory.* But this mark of *intrinsic* logical truth is only *negative;* for a cognition that contradicts itself is indeed false, but one that does not contradict itself is not always true.

Secondly, that it be *logically well-founded*, that is, that it (*a*) rest on principles, and (*b*) have no false consequences.

This second criterion of the *external* logical truth, or the *reasonableness* of a cognition, which concerns the logical, connexion of a cognition with principles and consequences, is *positive.* And here the following rules hold good:—

1°. From the *truth of the consequence* we may reason to the *truth* of the cognition as *its principle*, but only *negatively;* [221] viz. if one false consequence follows from a cognition, then the cognition itself is false. For if the principle were true, then the consequence would needs be true also, since the consequence is determined by the principle.

But we cannot conclude conversely; that if no false consequence follows from a cognition it is true; for from a false principle true consequences may be drawn.

2°. *If all the consequences of a cognition are true, then the cognition itself is true.* For if there were any falsity in the cognition, some false consequence must needs exist.

From the consequence, then, we may infer some principle, but without being able to determine what this principle is. It is only from the total of all consequences that we can reason to *a definite principle* that this is the true one.

The first mode of inference by which the consequence can only be a *negatively* and *indirectly* sufficient criterion of a cognition is called in Logic the *apagogic* mode (*modus tollens*).

This process, of which frequent use is made in geometry, has the advantage that, in order to prove a cognition false, I only require to draw a single false consequence from it. In order to show, for example, that the earth is not flat, I need not adduce any positive and direct reason; it is sufficient to reason indirectly and apagogically thus : if the earth were flat, the polestar would always appear at the same altitude; but this is not the case, therefore the earth is not flat.

In the other, the *positive* and *direct* method of proof (*modus ponens*), the difficulty occurs that the totality of consequences cannot be known apodictically, and that therefore by this method we arrive only at a probable and *hypothetically* true cognition (a hypothesis) ; on the supposition that where many consequences are true, the rest may also be true.

[222] We are able therefore to lay down here three principles as the universal merely formal or logical criteria of truth, namely :—

1°. *The Principle of Contradiction and of Identity* (*principium contradictionis* and *identitatis*) by which the intrinsic possibility of a cognition is determined for *problematical* judgments.

2°. *The Principle of Sufficient Reason* (*principium rationis sufficientis*) on which the (logical) *actuality* of a cognition depends; that it is well-founded, as material for *assertorial* judgments.

3°. *The Principle of Excluded Middle* (*principium exclusi medii inter duo contradictoria*) on which the (logical) necessity of a cognition is based, that we must necessarily judge thus and not otherwise, that is, that the contradictory is false. This is the principle of *apodictic* judgments.

The opposite of truth is Falsity, which when taken for truth is called Error. An erroneous judgment (for error as well as truth exists only in judgments) is therefore one which mistakes the appearance of truth for truth itself.

It is easy to see *how truth is possible*, since in it the understanding acts according to its own essential laws.

But *how error is possible in the formal sense of the word, that is, how a form of thought inconsistent with the understanding* is possible; this is hard to comprehend; as indeed in general we cannot comprehend how any faculty can deviate from its own essential laws. [223] We must not therefore look for the source of errors in the understanding itself and its essential laws, any more than in the *limits* of the understanding, in which indeed the cause of *ignorance* lies, but by no means that of error. Now if we had no faculty of knowledge except the understanding, we should never err. But besides the understanding there is in us another indispensable source of knowledge. This is the sensibility, which supplies the material for thought, and besides works according to different laws from the understanding. From the sensibility, however, considered in and by itself, error cannot arise, since the senses do not judge.

Hence the origin of all error must be sought solely in the *unobserved influence of the sensibility on the understanding*, or, to speak more exactly, on the *judgment*. It is owing to this influence that in our judgments we mistake merely *subjective* reasons for objective, and consequently confound the *mere semblance of truth* with *truth itself*. For it is just in this that the nature of semblance consists, which on this account is to be viewed as a reason for holding a false cognition to be true.

What makes error possible is therefore *semblance*, which occasions the confusion in judgment of the merely *subjective* with the *objective*.

We may indeed in a certain sense call the understanding

also the source of errors, inasmuch as from not sufficiently attending to that influence of the sensibility, it allows itself to be misled by the resulting semblance, so as to take subjective reasons for objective, or to regard as valid by its own laws that which is only true by the laws of the sensibility.

It follows that it is the fault of ignorance only that lies with the limits of the understanding; the fault of error we must attribute to ourselves. Nature has indeed denied us knowledge on many points; on much she leaves us in an inevitable ignorance, [224] but she is not the cause to us of error. To this we are misled by our own propensity to judge and to decide even where, on account of our limited capacities, we have not faculties to judge and to decide.

Every error, however, into which the human understanding can fall is only *partial*, and in every erring judgment there must always be contained some truth. For a *total* error would be a complete contradiction to the laws of the understanding and the reason. As such, how could it in any way come from the understanding, and being after all a judgment, be regarded as a product of the understanding?

With regard to what is true and erroneous in our cognition, we distinguish an *exact* from a *rough* knowledge.

The knowledge is *exact* when it corresponds to its object, or when in relation to its object there is not the smallest error; it is *rough* when it may include errors which do not interfere with its purpose.

This distinction concerns the *wider* or *narrower* determination of our knowledge (*cognitio late vel stricte determinata*). At first it is sometimes necessary to give a wider determination to a cognition, especially in historical matters. In rational cognitions everything ought to be exactly (*stricte*) determined. When the determination is wide, we say the cognition is determined *præter propter*. It always depends on the purpose of a cognition whether it is to be determined roughly or exactly. Wide determination always leaves some room for error, which, however, may have its definite limits. Error is especially wont to occur where a wide determination is taken for a strict one—for example, in questions of morality, in which everything must be strictly determined. [225] Those who do not attend to this are called by the English Latitudinarians.

Exactness, which is an objective perfection of knowledge—since the cognition then fully corresponds with the object—may be further distinguished from *subtilty*, which is a *subjective* perfection of knowledge.

A cognition of a thing is subtile when one discovers in it something that usually escapes the attention of others. Accordingly it requires a higher degree of attention, and a greater intellectual effort.

Many persons find fault with all subtilty because they cannot themselves attain it. But in itself it always does honour to the understanding, and is even meritorious and necessary when it is applied to an object deserving of observation. When, however, the same end might have been attained with less attention and effort of the understanding, and yet one exerts more, then one expends useless effort, and falls into subtilties which, though difficult, are useless (*nugæ difficiles*).

As rough is opposed to exact, so is *coarse* opposed to *subtile*.

From the nature of error, the conception of which, as we have observed, includes as an essential element besides falsity the appearance of truth, there results the following important rule for the truth of our knowledge. In order to avoid errors—and no error is absolutely *unavoidable*, although it may be *relatively* so in cases where we cannot avoid judging even at the risk of falling into error—in order, then, to avoid errors we must try to discover and explain their source, namely, semblance. [226] Few philosophers, however, have done this. They have only endeavoured to refute the errors themselves without pointing out the semblance from which they arise. Yet this detection and solution of semblance is a far more important service to truth than the direct refutation of the errors themselves, by which we cannot stop up their source, or prevent the same semblance from again leading to error, since it is undetected.

For even when we are convinced that we have erred, yet when the semblance, which is the foundation of our error, is not removed, there still remain *scruples*, however little we can produce to justify them.

Further, by explanation of the semblance a kind of justice is done to the person in error. For no one will admit that he has erred without some appearance of truth which might perhaps have deceived even a more acute person, since in such matters subjective reasons count for something.

An error in which the semblance is evident even to common sense (*sensus communis*) is called an *absurdity*. The charge of absurdity is always a personal reproach which we must avoid, especially in refuting errors. For when a man maintains an absurdity, the semblance which is the source of this evident falsity is not evident to him. We must first *make* it evident to him. If he still abides by his error, then no doubt he is absurd, but then we can do no more with him. He has thereby made himself both incapable and unworthy of all correction and refutation. For we cannot *prove* to anyone that he is absurd; all reasoning would be thrown away on this. [227] When we prove the absurdity then we no longer reason with a man in error, but with a rational man. But then the detection of the absurdity (*deductio ad absurdum*) is unnecessary.

We may also call an error *absurd* when it is not excused by anything, *not even by semblance;* as a *gross* error is one which shows ignorance in matters of common knowledge, or offends against common observation.

Error in *principles* is more important than error *in their application.*

An *external* mark, or an *external* touchstone of truth is the comparison of our own judgment with that of others, since what is subjective cannot exist alike in all others, and hence semblance may be thus cleared up. The *inconsistency* of the judgment of others with our own is therefore to be regarded as an external mark of error, and as a hint that we should examine how we have arrived at our judgment, but not therefore to reject it at once; for we may perhaps be right *in substance*, and wrong only *in the manner* of representing it.

Common sense (*sensus communis*) is also in itself a touchstone for detecting the errors of the *technical* use of the understanding. When we use common sense as a test of the correctness of the speculative understanding, we are said to fix our bearings by common sense.

General rules and conditions of the avoidance of error are—1° to think oneself; 2° to put oneself in thought in the place or point of view of another; and 3° always to think consistently. [228] The first may be called *enlightened;* the second *enlarged;* and the third *consequent* or *coherent thinking.*

VIII.

C.—*Logical Perfection of Knowledge as to Quality—Clearness— Conception of an Attribute generally—Different kinds of Attributes—Definition of the Logical Essence of a Thing— Distinction of this from the Real Essence—Distinctness a higher Degree of Clearness—Aesthetic and Logical Distinctness—Distinction between Analytical and Synthetical Distinctness.*

Human knowledge is on the side of the understanding *discursive;* that is, it takes place by means of ideas which make what is common to many things the ground of knowledge; and hence, by means of attributes as such. We therefore cognise things only *by means of attributes.*

An attribute is that in a thing which constitutes part of our cognition of it; or, what is the same, *a partial conception so far as it is considered as a ground of cognition of the whole conception.* All our Concepts, therefore, are attributes, and all Thought is nothing but conception by means of attributes.

Every attribute may be considered in two aspects—

First, as a conception in itself.

Secondly, as a partial concept, forming part of the whole conception of a thing, and thereby as a ground of cognition of this thing itself.

[229] All attributes considered as grounds of cognition are of *twofold* use, either *internal* or *external*. The *internal* use consists in *derivation*, in order to cognise the thing itself by means of attributes as grounds of cognition. The external use consists in *comparison*, inasmuch as by means of attributes we can compare one thing with another, according to the rules of Identity or Diversity.

There are several specific distinctions between attributes, on which the following classification of them is based:—

1°. Analytic or Synthetic attributes. The former are partial conceptions of my *actual* concept (which I already think in it); the latter, on the contrary, are partial conceptions of the *merely possible* total concept (which therefore is to be the result of a synthesis of several parts). The former are all rational concepts; the latter may be concepts of experience.

2°. Co-ordinate or Subordinate. This division of attributes relates to their connexion with one another.

Attributes are *co-ordinate* when each of them is conceived as an immediate attribute of the thing; they are subordinate when one attribute is conceived as belonging to the thing only by means of another. The combination of co-ordinate attributes into the whole of the concept is called an *aggregate;* the combination of subordinate attributes is called a *series.* The former, the aggregation of co-ordinate attributes, constitutes the totality of the concept, which however in the case of synthetic empirical concepts can never be completed, but is like an *unlimited* straight line.

The series of subordinate attributes touches *a parte ante,* or on the side of the reasons, upon insoluble concepts which on account of their simplicity cannot be further analysed; [230] on the other hand *a parte post,* or with regard to the consequences, it is *unlimited, since we can have a highest genus, but not a lowest species*.

With the synthesis of every new concept in the aggregation of co-ordinate attributes the *extensive* distinctness is increased; and with the further analysis of the concept in the series of subordinated attributes the *intensive* distinctness is increased. Since this latter kind of distinctness essentially promotes the *thoroughness* and coherence of the cognition it is especially the business of philosophy, and is pushed farthest in metaphysical inquiries in particular.

3°. Positive and Negative attributes. By the former we learn what the thing is; by the latter what it is not.

Negative attributes serve to keep us from errors. Hence they are *unnecessary where it is impossible to err*, and are only necessary and important in those cases where they keep us from an important error into which we might readily fall. Thus, for instance, with respect to the concept of a Divine Being, the negative attributes are very necessary and important. By means of positive attributes, then, we *understand* a thing; by means of negative—in which form all attributes may be expressed—we only do not *misunderstand* it or do not *err* in it, although we should not thereby learn to know anything.

4°. Important and fruitful, or Unimportant and useless attributes.

An attribute is important and fruitful when it is a ground of knowledge of great and important consequences, *partly* with respect to its intrinsic employment—its employment in derivation—that is, so far as it enables us to know a good deal of the thing itself; partly with respect to its external employment—its employment in comparison—in so far as it enables us to recognise both the similarity of a thing to many others, and its dissimilarity to many others.

[231] We must distinguish further under this head the *logical* importance and fruitfulness from the *practical*, viz. *profitableness* and *utility*.

5°. Adequate and essential, or Inadequate and contingent attributes.

An attribute is *adequate* when it suffices to distinguish the thing in every case from all others; if not, it is inadequate, as for instance the attribute barking of a dog. The adequacy of attributes, however, as well as their importance, is to be decided only relatively with relation to the end to be attained by knowledge.

Essential attributes are those which must always be found in the thing conceived. These are opposed to *non-essential* and contingent attributes, which can be separated from the concept of the thing.

Amongst essential attributes there is a further distinction. Some belong to the thing as the causes of other attributes of the same thing; others, on the contrary, only as the *consequences* of other attributes. The former are *primitive* and *constitutive* attributes (*constitutiva, essentialia in sensu strictissimo*); the others are *derivative* (*consectaria, rationata*), and belong indeed to the nature of the thing, but only inasmuch as they follow from its essential elements; *ex. gr.* the three angles of a triangle from the three sides.

The *non-essential* attributes again are twofold; they concern either the *internal* characters of a thing (*modi*), or its *external* relations (*relationes*). [232] Thus learning is an internal character of man; *to be master or servant* is only an external relation.

The totality of all the essential elements of a thing, or the adequacy of its attributes in respect of co-ordination or subordination, is its Essence (*complexus notarum primitivarum, interne conceptui dato sufficientium ; s. complexus notarum, conceptum aliquem primitive constituentium*).

In this definition, however, we must by no means think of the *real* or *natural essence* of the thing, which we are wholly unable to discover. For since Logic abstracts from all content of knowledge, and consequently from the thing itself, this science can only be concerned with the *logical* essence of things. And this we can easily discern. For to do so only requires the knowledge of all the predicates with respect to which an object is determined *by its concept;* whereas the real essence of the thing (*esse rei*) would require the knowledge of those predicates on which everything that belongs to its existence depends. Would we, for instance, determine the logical essence of body, we need not search out the data for this in nature; we need only reflect on the attributes which as essential elements (*constitutiva, rationes*) originally constitute the fundamental conception of it. For the logical essence is nothing but *the first fundamental conception of all the essential attributes of a thing* (*esse conceptus*).

[233] The first degree, then, of perfection of our knowledge as to quality is its clearness. A second or a higher degree of clearness is Distinctness. This consists in the *clearness of attributes.*

We must first distinguish logical from aesthetic distinctness in general. Logical distinctness rests on the objective, aesthetic on the subjective clearness of attributes. The former is a clearness by means of *concepts,* the latter a clearness by means of *intuition.* The latter kind of distinctness, then, consists in a mere *vividness* and *intelligibility,* that is, in a mere clearness by means of examples *in concreto* (for much may be intelligible which is not distinct, and conversely much may be distinct which is yet hard to understand, because it reaches back to remote attributes, the connexion of which with intuition is only possible through a long series).

Objective distinctness often causes subjective obscurity, and *vice versa.* Hence logical distinctness is not seldom possible only at the expense of aesthetic distinctness, and conversely aesthetic distinctness often injures logical distinctness by means of examples and similitudes which do not exactly fit, but are only adopted by analogy. Besides, examples are not attributes, and are no part of the concept, but only belong as intuitions to the employment of the concept. Distinctness by means of examples—mere intelligibility—is therefore of a quite different kind from distinctness by means of concepts which are attributes.

The combination of the two, the aesthetic or popular, and the scholastic or logical distinctness, constitutes Lucidity. For by a *lucid intellect* we understand the talent of presenting abstract and profound matters of knowledge in a luminous manner, adapted to the capacity of ordinary men.

[234] Now as regards logical distinctness in particular, this is to be called a *complete* distinctness when all the attributes which taken together constitute the whole concept have arrived at clearness. A concept, again, may be completely or thoroughly distinct either in respect of the totality of its *co-ordinate*, or in respect of the totality of its *subordinate* attributes. The total clearness of the co-ordinate attributes constitutes the *extensively* complete or adequate distinctness of a concept, which is also called Fulness. The total clearness of the subordinate attributes constitutes *intensively* complete distinctness—Profundity. The former kind of logical distinctness may also be called *external completeness (completudo externa)*, while the other may be called the *internal completeness* of the clearness of the attributes. The latter can be attained only in pure rational concepts, and arbitrary concepts, not in concepts of experience.

In the extensive quantity of distinctness absence of superfluity is called Precision.   Completeness *(completudo)* and Precision *(praecisio)* together constitute Adequacy *(cognitionem quae rem adaequat)* ; and *intensive adequacy* in profundity, joined with extensive adequacy in fulness and precision, constitute (as regards Quality) the consummate perfection of a cognition *(consummata cognitionis perfectio)*.

Now since, as we have remarked, it is the business of Logic *to make clear concepts distinct*, the question arises, *in what manner* it makes them distinct ?

[235] According to the logicians of Wolff's school it is only by analysis of cognitions that they are made distinct. But it is not in all cases that distinctness rests on the analysis of a given concept. Analysis gives distinctness only with respect to those attributes which we have already thought in the concept, but not at all in reference to those attributes which are added to

the concept as parts of the entire possible concept. That kind of distinctness which arises not by virtue of analysis, but by synthesis of attributes is synthetic distinctness. There is then an essential difference between the two statements: *to make a distinct concept*, and *to make a concept distinct*.·

For when I make a distinct concept I begin from the parts and proceed from these to the whole. There are in this case no attributes present; I obtain them first by the synthesis. From this synthetic process, then, results synthetic distinctness, which actually enlarges the comprehension of my concept by that which *over and above* it is added as attribute in intuition (whether pure or empirical). This synthetic process of making distinct concepts is employed by the mathematician, and also by the natural philosopher. For in every instance the distinctness of properly mathematical cognitions, as well as of cognitions of experience, depends on such an enlargement of them by means of synthesis of attributes.

But when I make a concept distinct, then by this, which is mere analysis, my knowledge is not increased as to its comprehension. This remains the same; only the form is changed, inasmuch as what already was contained in the given concept I now learn to distinguish better, or to recognize with clear consciousness. Just as by mere illumination of a map nothing is added to it, so by the mere clearing up of a given concept by analysis of its attributes this concept itself is not in the least degree enlarged.

[236] It is the part of synthesis to make the objects distinct; that of analysis to make the concepts distinct. In the latter case the whole precedes the parts; in the former, the parts precede the whole. The philosopher only makes given concepts distinct. Sometimes we proceed synthetically even when the concept which we desire in this way to make distinct is already *given*. This is often the case with empirical propositions when one is not contented with the attributes already thought in a given concept.

The analytical method of producing distinctness, with which alone Logic can concern itself, is the first and chief requirement in making our knowledge distinct. For the more distinct our knowledge of a thing is, the stronger and more effective it can be, only the analysis must not go so far that at last the object itself disappears.

If we were conscious of everything that we know, we should be amazed at the great number of our cognitions.

With respect to the objective value of our knowledge in general we may conceive the following *degrees* :—

The first degree of knowledge is : *to have an idea* of a thing [sich etwas vorstellen].

The second : consciously to have an idea of a thing, or to perceive it (*percipere*).

The third : to *know* a thing (*noscere*), or to have an idea of a thing in comparison with other things both as regards Identity and Diversity.

[237] The fourth: *consciously* to know a thing, that is, to *cognise* it (*cognoscere*). Animals *know* objects but do not *cognise* them.

The fifth : to *understand* (*intelligere*), that is, to cognise it *by the understanding by means of concepts*, or to *conceive* it. This is very different from *comprehending* it. There are many things which we can conceive without being able to comprehend them, *ex. gr.* a *perpetuum mobile*, the impossibility of which is proved in Mechanics.

The sixth is : to cognise or *discern* something by the reason (*perspicere*). We have attained to this degree in very few things, and our cognitions become fewer and fewer the more we wish to perfect them in intrinsic value.

Finally, the seventh degree is : to *comprehend* a thing (*comprehendere*), that is, to cognise it by the reason, or *à priori*, in such a degree as is adequate to our purpose. For all our comprehension is only *relative*, that is, adequate to a certain purpose —we cannot *absolutely* comprehend anything. Nothing can be more completely comprehended than what the mathematician demonstrates, *ex. gr.* that all lines in a circle are proportional.

And yet he does not comprehend how it happens that so simple a figure has these properties. Hence, the field of the Understanding is far wider than the field of the Reason, or of Comprehension.

IX.

D.—*Logical Perfection of Knowledge as to Modality—Certainty— Notion of Assent in General—Modes of Assent : Opinion, Belief, Knowledge—Conviction and Persuasion—Reserve and Suspension of Judgment—Provisional Judgments— Prejudices : their Sources and different Kinds.*

Truth is an *objective* property of knowledge ; but the judgment by which a thing is *thought* as true—and which has reference to an understanding, and therefore to a special thinking subject—is *subjective ;* it is Assent.

Assent in general is of two kinds : *certain* or *uncertain.* Certain assent, or Certainty, is joined with consciousness of necessity ; the uncertain on the contrary, or *Uncertainty,* is joined with the consciousness of contingency, or the possibility of the opposite. The latter, again, is either *subjectively as well as objectively inadequate ;* or it is *objectively inadequate,* but *subjectively adequate.* The former must be called Opinion, the latter Belief. There are, then, three sorts or modes (*modi*) of assent : Opinion, Belief, and Knowledge. Opinion is a *problematical,* Belief an *assertorial,* and Knowledge an *apodictic* judging. For what I hold merely as opinion, this in judging I consciously regard as only *problematical ;* what I believe, I regard as *assertorial,* not however as objectively, but as subjectively necessary (valid only for me) ; finally, what I *know,* I regard as *apodictically certain,* that is, as universally and objectively necessary (valid for all) ; [239] supposing even that the object itself to which this certain assent relates were a mere empirical truth. For this distinction of assent, according to the three just mentioned modes, concerns only the Faculty of Judgment with respect to the subjective criteria for the subsumption of a judgment under objective rules.

Thus, for instance, our assent to the immortality of the soul would be merely problematical in case we only act as if we were immortal; assertorial, in case we believe that we are immortal; and lastly, apodictic, in case we *all* knew that there is another life after this.

Hence, there is an essential difference between opinion, belief, and knowledge, which we shall now expound with more exactness and detail.

I. *Opinion.*—Opinion or assent from a reason which is neither subjectively nor objectively adequate may be also regarded as a *provisional* judging (*sub conditione suspensiva ad interim*) with which we cannot readily dispense. We must first hold as opinion before we assume and assert, but we must take care not to take an opinion as more than mere opinion. In all our knowledge we begin for the most part from opinion. Sometimes we have an obscure presentiment of the truth; a thing seems to us to contain marks of truth; we *suspect* the truth even before we recognise it with definite certainty.

Now what is the proper sphere of mere opinion? Not in any sciences that contain *à priori* cognitions; therefore not in mathematics, nor in metaphysics, nor in ethics, but only in *empirical* branches of knowledge, in physics, psychology, and the like. For it is in itself absurd to have an opinion *à priori*. And in fact nothing could be more ridiculous than, *ex. gr.* in mathematics, to have a mere opinion. In this science, as also in metaphysics and ethics, the rule holds—*either we know, or we do not know*. [240] It is, therefore, only the objects of empirical knowledge that can be matters of opinion—a knowledge that *in itself* indeed is possible, but only *for us* impossible from the empirical limitations and conditions of our faculty of experience, and the particular degree of this faculty that we possess, and which depends on these conditions. Thus, for instance, the Ether of modern physicists is a mere matter of opinion. For in the case of this, as well as every opinion generally, whatever it may be, I perceive that the opposite might possibly admit of proof. My assent, then, in this case is both objectively and subjectively inadequate ; although considered in itself, it may be complete.

II. *Belief.*—Belief or assent from a reason which is objectively inadequate, but subjectively adequate, relates to objects with respect to which we not only can know nothing, but also can have no opinion—nay, cannot even allege probability, but only can be certain that it is not contradictory to conceive such objects in the way in which we do conceive them. The rest is a *free* assent, which is only necessary in a practical *à priori* point of view ; an assent, therefore, to that which I assume from *moral* grounds, and so that I am certain that the *opposite* can never be proved. [1]

[241] Amongst matters of belief, then, are 1°, no objects of *empirical* knowledge. [242] The so-called historical belief cannot therefore be properly called belief, or contrasted as such

---

[1] Belief is not a special source of knowledge. It is a kind of consciously imperfect assent, and when it is considered as restricted to a particular class of objects (with which alone belief is concerned), it differs from opinion not in degree, but by the relation that it has to action. Thus, for instance, a merchant in order to enter upon a business transaction requires not merely the opinion that something is to be gained by it, but the belief, that is, his opinion must be firm enough to run the risk. Now we have theoretical cognitions (of sensible things) in which we can attain certainty, and this must be possible with respect to everything that we can call human knowledge. [241] Just such certain knowledge, and that too wholly *à priori*, we have in practical laws, but these are based on a supersensible principle (that of freedom), and one that is *within ourselves*, being a principle of practical reason. But this practical reason is a causality with respect to an object which is likewise supersensible, the supreme good, which is not attainable by our faculties in the sensible world. Nevertheless, nature, as the object of our theoretical reason, must agree therewith ; for the *consequence* or *effect* of this idea must be met with in the sensible world. We ought, therefore, so to act as to make this end actual.

We find, also, in the sensible world traces of Designing Wisdom, and hence we believe that the cause of the world operates also with *moral* wisdom towards the supreme good. This is an assent which is sufficient for action, that is, a Belief. Now we do not require this for action according to moral laws ; for these are given solely by practical reason ; but we require the assumption of a supreme wisdom as

with knowledge, since it may itself be knowledge. Assent on testimony does not differ either in degree or in kind from assent from our own experience.

2°. No objects of rational knowledge (knowledge *à priori*) are matters of belief, whether their knowledge be theoretical, *ex. gr.* in mathematics and metaphysics, or practical in morals.

[243] We may indeed believe mathematical truths, which are rational, on testimony, partly because in this sphere error is not readily possible, partly also because it can be readily detected ; but we cannot in this fashion have knowledge. Philosophical truths, however, which are rational, cannot be matters of belief at all ; they must simply be known ; for philosophy does not admit of any mere persuasion. And as regards the objects of practical rational knowledge in morals, rights and duties, just as little can there be mere belief in their case. One must be *thoroughly certain* whether a thing is right or wrong, according to, or contrary to duty, permitted or forbidden. Nothing can be ventured in moral matters on an uncertainty ;

---

the object of our moral will, an object to which (besides the mere correctness of our actions) we cannot avoid directing our ends. Although *objectively* this would not be a necessary reference of our elective will ; yet the supreme good is the *subjectively* necessary object of a good (even human) will, and the belief in its attainability is a necessary presupposition.

There is no mean between the acquisition of a cognition by experience (*à posteriori*) and by reason (*à priori*). But between the cognition of an object and the mere presupposition of its possibility there is a mean, namely, a ground from reason or experience for assuming the latter in relation to a necessary enlargement of the field of possible objects beyond those the knowledge of which is possible for us. This necessity exists only where the object is recognised by the reason as practical and practically necessary, for the assumption of a thing for the purpose of enlargement of theoretical knowledge is always contingent. This practically necessary supposition of an object is that of the possibility of the supreme good as an object of elective will, and hence also of the condition of this possibility (God, Freedom, and Immortality). This is a subjective necessity to assume the reality of the object for the sake of the necessary determination of the will. This is the *casus extraordinarius*, without which practical reason cannot maintain itself in respect of its necessary end, and here the *favor necessitatis* comes to help it in its own judgment. [242] It cannot logically attain any object, but only can resist whatever hinders it in the employment of this idea which practically belongs to it.

This belief is the necessity of assuming the objective reality of a concept (of the

nothing resolved *at the risk of offending the law.* Thus, for example, it is not enough for a judge that he should *merely believe* that the man accused of a crime has actually committed it ; he must (judicially) know it, else he acts unconscientiously.

3°. Those objects alone are matters of belief in which assent is necessarily free, that is, is not determined by objective reasons independent on the nature and interest of the subject.

Belief, therefore, on account of its merely subjective reasons, does not give a conviction that can be communicated to others, or command universal assent, like the conviction that comes from knowledge. Only I, myself, can be certain of the validity and the unchangeableness of my practical belief ; and my belief in the truth of a proposition, or the actuality of a thing, is that which in relation to me takes the place of a cognition without being itself a cognition.

That man is morally *unbelieving* who does not accept that which, though *impossible* to know, is *morally necessary* to suppose. [244] A want of moral interest always lies at the root of this kind of unbelief. The higher the moral character of a man, the more firm and vivid will be his belief in everything which

---

supreme good), that is, the possibility of its object as an object of elective will, necessary *à priori.* If we merely look to actions, then this belief is not necessary. But if we would by actions raise ourselves to the possession of the end thereby made possible, then we must suppose that this is quite possible. I can only say, then : I see myself compelled by my end, following laws of freedom, to suppose a supreme good in the world as possible, but I cannot compel any others by reasons (belief is *free*).

Rational belief, then, can never reach to theoretical knowledge ; for in theoretical matters an objectively inadequate assent is merely Opinion. It is only a supposition of the reason in a subjective but absolutely necessary practical point of view. The mental disposition which accords with moral laws leads to an object of elective will, determinable by pure reason. The assumption of the feasibility of this object, and therefore also of the actuality of its cause, is a *moral* or free belief, and in the moral point of view of the fulfilment of its end it is a necessary assent.

Fides is properly faithfulness *in pacto,* or subjective trust in one another, that one will keep his promise to the other—*Faith* and *Credit.* The former when the *pactum* has been made ; the latter when it is about to be made.

Speaking by way of analogy, the practical reason is, as it were, the *promiser*, man is the *promisee*, and the good expected from the act is the *promissum*.

he feels himself compelled from moral interest to accept and suppose in a practically necessary point of view.

III. *Knowledge.*—Assent from a reason which is both subjectively and objectively adequate, or Certainty, is either Empirical or Rational, according as it is based on Experience— our own or others'—or on Reason. This distinction, then, has reference to the two sources from which all our knowledge is derived—Experience and Reason.

Rational certainty, again, is either mathematical or philosophical certainty. The former is Intuitive, the latter Discursive.

Mathematical certainty is also called Evidence, because an intuitive cognition is clearer than a discursive. Although, then, both mathematical and philosophical knowledge are equally certain, yet the kind of certainty in the two is different.

Empirical certainty is original (*originarie empirica*) when it is founded on my own experience; it is derived (*derivative empirica*) when founded on that of others. This latter is also commonly called *historical* certainty.

Rational certainty differs from empirical by the consciousness of *necessity* that is connected with it; it is therefore an *apodictic* certainty, whereas empirical certainty is only *assertorial*. We are rationally certain of that which even without experience we should have discerned *à priori*. [245] Hence it is possible that our cognitions may concern objects of experience and yet their certainty may be both empirical and rational, namely, when we discern from *à priori* principles the truth of a proposition which is empirically certain.

We cannot have rational certainty of everything; but wherever we can have it we must prefer it to the empirical.

All certainty is either *immediate* or *mediate*, that is, either it needs proof, or it neither requires nor admits proof. Although there be never so much in our knowledge that is only mediately certain, that is, only by means of proof, yet there must be something *indemonstrable* or *immediately certain*, and all our knowledge must proceed from propositions *immediately certain*.

The proofs on which all certainty, mediate or immediate, depends, are either *direct* or *indirect*, that is *apagogic*. When I prove a truth from the reasons of it, I adduce a direct proof of it ; and when I infer the truth of a proposition from the falsity of its opposite, I use an apagogic proof. In order, however, that this latter reasoning should be valid, the propositions must be *contradictories* or *diametrically* opposed. For two merely contrary propositions (*contrarie opposita*) may be both false.

A proof which is the ground of mathematical certainty is called Demonstration, and one which is the ground of philosophical certainty is an Acroamatic proof. The essential elements of every proof are Matter and Form ; or the Premisses and the Sequence.

From "knowing" is derived the name Science ["Wissenschaft" from "Wissen"], by which is meant the whole content of a cognition as a System. Science is contrasted with *common* knowledge, that is, the content of a cognition, as a mere Aggregate. [246] System rests on an idea of the whole, which precedes the parts; whereas, in common knowledge, or the mere aggregate of cognitions, the parts precede the whole. There are Historical sciences and Rational sciences.

In a science we often *know* only the *cognitions*, and not the *things represented* by them, so that there may be a science of that, our cognition of which is not knowledge.

From the preceding remarks on the nature and kinds of assent, we may now draw the general result—that all our convictions are either *logical* or *practical*. In fact, when we know that we are not influenced by any subjective reasons, and yet the assent is adequate, then we are *convinced*, and moreover *logically* or from *objective* reasons (the object is certain).

Complete assent from subjective reasons which, for *practical purposes*, are as valid as objective, is also conviction, only not logical but *practical* (*I am certain*). And this practical conviction, or *moral rational belief*, is often firmer than any knowledge.   In the case of knowledge one listens to counter reasons, but not in that of belief; because this turns not on objective reasons, but on the moral interest of the subject.[1]

[247] Conviction is opposed to Persuasion, which is an assent from inadequate reasons, of which we do not know whether they are only subjective or are also objective.

Persuasion often precedes conviction.   Of many cognitions we are conscious only in such a manner as not to be able to judge whether the grounds of our assent are objective or subjective.   Hence, in order to be able to advance from persuasion to conviction, we must first *reflect*, that is, see to what faculty a cognition belongs; and then *investigate*, that is, try whether the grounds are, in relation to the object, adequate or inadequate. Many do not get beyond persuasion.   Some go as far as reflection; few reach investigation.   The man that knows what belongs to certainty will not readily confound conviction and persuasion, nor will he allow himself to be readily persuaded. Assent is sometimes determined by a mixture of objective and subjective grounds; and most men never separate the combined effect of these.

Although persuasion is always in form (*formaliter*) false— namely, because in it an uncertain cognition seems to be certain —yet in matter (*materialiter*) it may be true.   And it differs in this respect from opinion, which is an uncertain cognition *held as uncertain*.

The sufficiency of assent (in the case of belief) may be put

---

[1] This practical conviction, then, is the *moral rational belief* which alone is called in the strictest sense belief, and as such must be contrasted with knowledge, and with all theoretical or logical conviction, because it never can be raised to knowledge.   The so-called historical belief, on the contrary, as already remarked, should not be distinguished from knowledge, because being a kind of theoretical or logical assent it may itself be knowledge.   We may accept an empirical truth on the testimony of others with the same certainty as if we had obtained it by facts of our own experience.   [247] In the former kind of empirical knowledge we may be deceived, but so we may also in the latter.

Historical or mediate empirical knowledge rests on the trustworthiness of the testimony.   What is required in an unexceptionable witness is authenticity (competency) and integrity.

to the test by *wager* or by *oath*. [248] The former requires *comparative*, the latter *absolute* sufficiency of objective reasons, instead of which, when they are not present, an assent which is only subjectively adequate is held to be sufficient.

We often hear the expressions : *to adopt a judgment ; to reserve, suspend,* or *surrender our judgment.* These and similar phrases seem to imply that there is something voluntary in our judgments, inasmuch as we regard something as true because we wish to do so. The question, then, arises : *Has the will any influence on our judgments ?* The will has no immediate influence on assent; this would be very absurd. When it is said, *we easily believe what we wish,* this refers only to our kindly wishes, *ex. gr.* those of a father for his children. If the will had an immediate influence on our conviction of what we wish, we should constantly frame chimerical notions of good fortune, and always regard them as true. But the will cannot contend *against* convincing proofs of truths which are adverse to its wishes and inclinations.

Inasmuch, however, as the will either urges the understanding to the examination of a truth, or withholds it therefrom, we must allow it an influence on the *employment* of the understanding, and hence, indirectly, on conviction itself, as this depends so much on the employment of the understanding. As to the *suspension* or *reserve* of our judgment in particular, this consists in the resolution not to allow a merely *provisional* judgment to become a definitive one. A provisional judgment is one by which I represent to myself that there are more reasons *for* the truth of a thing than *against* it ; [249] but that these reasons are not sufficient for a definitive judgment by which I should decide positively for its truth. Provisional judgment, therefore, is that which is consciously problematical. Reservation of judgment may take place with a twofold purpose—either in order to examine the reasons for a definitive judgment, or in order *never* to decide. In the former case the suspension of judgment is called *critical* (*suspensio judicii indagatoria*) ; in the latter it is *sceptical* (*suspensio judicii sceptica*). For the sceptic despairs of judgment altogether; the true philosopher, on the contrary, only suspends his judgment when he has not yet sufficient reasons for holding a thing to be true.

The suspension of one's judgment *on principle* requires a practised faculty which is only found in advanced years. On the whole, it is a difficult thing to reserve our assent, partly because our understanding is so eager to extend itself by judgments, and to enrich itself with cognitions, partly because our inclination is always directed more to some things than to others. But the man who has often had to reverse his assent, and has thereby become prudent and cautious, will not so quickly grant it, fearing lest he should afterwards be obliged to retract his judgment. This *retractation* is always mortifying, and leads a man to mistrust all other cognitions.

We remark, further, that to leave our judgment *in dubio* is not the same as to leave it *in suspenso*. In the latter case I always have an interest in the thing ; in the former it does not always suit my end and my interest to decide whether the thing is true or not.

Provisional judgments are very necessary—nay, indispensable for the employment of the understanding in all meditation and inquiry ; [250] for they serve to guide the understanding in its inquiries, and to supply it with various means thereto.

When we meditate on a thing we must always form a provisional judgment, and, as it were, scent out the cognition which we are to attain by meditation. And when we are on the look out for inventions or discoveries we must always make a provisional plan, otherwise our thoughts go on at random. We may, therefore, by provisional judgments, understand *maxims* for the inquiry into a thing. They may also be called *anticipations*, because we anticipate our judgment of a thing before we have a definitive judgment. Such judgments, then, have their use, and there might even be given rules how to form provisional judgments.

Prejudices must be distinguished from provisional judgments. Prejudices are provisional judgments that are *adopted as principles.*   Every prejudice is to be viewed as a principle of erroneous judgments, and from prejudices arise not prejudices, but erroneous judgments. We must, therefore, distinguish from the prejudice itself the false cognition that arises from the prejudice.   Thus, for instance, the significance of dreams is in itself not a prejudice, but an error that arises from the assumed general rule—that what sometimes happens always happens, or is always to be regarded as true.   And this principle, to which the significance of dreams is to be referred, is a prejudice.

Sometimes prejudices are true provisional judgments ; only it is not right that they should take the place of principles or definitive judgments.   [251] The cause of this delusion is that subjective reasons are falsely regarded as objective from *want of reflexion*, which ought to precede all judgment.   For while we may accept many cognitions, *ex. gr.* the immediately certain propositions, without *examining* them, that is, without testing the conditions of their truth, yet we cannot and ought not to form a judgment about anything without *reflecting*, that is, without comparing a cognition with the faculty from which it is supposed to rise (the sensibility or the understanding). If we adopt judgments without this reflexion, which is necessary even where there is no *examination*, then prejudices arise, or principles of judging from subjective causes, which are wrongly taken for objective reasons.

The chief sources of prejudices are : Imitation, Custom, and Inclination.

Imitation has a general influence on our judgments ; for we are strongly impelled to take that as true which others have alleged as true.   Hence the prejudice : what everyone does is right.   As to prejudices which have arisen from custom, these can be eradicated only by length of time, namely, while the understanding being by degrees checked and retarded in its judgments by counter reasons, is thereby gradually brought to an opposite tone of thought.   If, however, a prejudice of custom has also arisen from imitation, then the man that is possessed by it can hardly be cured of it.   A prejudice from imitation may also be called a *propensity to the passive employment of the reason*, or *to the mechanical use of the reason instead of its sponta-neous action in conformity with laws.*

Reason is an active principle which ought not to borrow anything from mere authority of others—nay, not even from experience, in cases where the *pure* use of reason is concerned. But the indolence of very many persons makes them prefer to tread in the footsteps of others rather than to exert their own understandings. [252] Such persons can never be anything but copies of others, and if all men were of this sort the world would for ever remain in one and the same place. It is, therefore, highly necessary and important not to confine the young, as is commonly done, to mere imitation.

There are many things that contribute to habituate us to the maxim of imitation, and thus to make the reason a fruitful soil of prejudices. Amongst these are :—

1°. *Formulas.*—These are rules, the expression of which serves as a pattern for imitation. They are, besides, extremely useful in simplifying involved sentences, and therefore the most en-lightened intellect endeavours to frame the like.

2°. *Sayings*, the expression of which has a great precision of pregnant sense, so that it seems as if one could not express the sense with fewer words. Sayings of this kind (*dicta*), which must always be borrowed from others to whom we ascribe a certain infallibility, serve, on account of this authority, as rule and law. The sayings of the Bible are called sayings κατ' ἐξοχήν.

3°. *Apophthegms*, that is, sentences that recommend them-selves, and often maintain their reputation for centuries, as products of a ripe judgment, by the striking effect of the thoughts they contain.

4°. *Canons.*—These are general aphorisms which serve as a basis to the sciences, and involve something lofty and well thought out. These may also be expressed in the manner of apophthegms that they may please the more.

5°. *Proverbs.*—These are popular rules of common sense or expressions to mark the popular judgment thereof. [253] As such merely provincial sayings only serve the common people as apophthegms and canons, they are not to be met with amongst persons of more refined education.

From the three sources of prejudices previously mentioned, and especially from imitation, there arise many peculiar prejudices, amongst which we will here touch on the following as the most usual:—

1°. Prejudices of Authority. In these we reckon:

(*a*) *The Prejudice of Personal Authority.*—When, in matters that depend on experience and testimony, we build our knowledge on the authority of other persons, we are not thereby involved in any prejudice; for in things of this sort, since we cannot ourselves experience everything, or embrace everything with our own understanding, personal authority must be the foundation of our judgments. But when we make the authority of others the ground of our assent with respect to rational cognitions, then we accept these cognitions from mere prejudice. For truths of reason hold good anonymously: with them it is not the question, *Who* has said it? but, *What* has he said? It is no matter whether a cognition is of noble origin; nevertheless the propensity to follow the authority of great men is very common, partly from the limitation of one's own insight, and partly from the desire to imitate what is described to us as *great*. To this is added, that personal authority serves in an indirect way to flatter our vanity. Just as the subjects of a powerful despot are proud that they are all treated *alike* by him, inasmuch as the lowest may imagine himself equal to the highest, because in presence of the unlimited power of their ruler they are both nothing; [254] so also the admirers of a great man regard themselves as equal, inasmuch as the advantages which one might have over another are to be esteemed insignificant in presence of the merits of the great man. For more than one reason, then, the much admired great men give no small impulse to the propensity to the prejudice of personal authority.

(*b*) *The Prejudice of Authority of the Majority.*—The vulgar are most inclined to this prejudice. For as they are not able to estimate the merits, the capacities, and the knowledge of the person, they attach themselves rather to the judgment of the majority, on the supposition that what everyone says must be true. However, this prejudice refers with them only to historical things; in matters of religion, in which they are themselves interested, they rely on the judgment of the learned.

In general it is remarkable that the ignorant man has a prejudice in favour of learning, and the learned man, on the contrary, a prejudice for common sense.

When the man of learning, after he has pretty well gone through the circle of the sciences, finds that all his labours have not procured due satisfaction, then at last he acquires a distrust of learning, especially in those speculations in which the concepts cannot be made sensible, and the foundations of which are unsettled, as, for instance, in metaphysics. Since, however, he believes that the key to certainty on some subjects is surely to be found somewhere, he seeks it now in common sense, having so long sought it in vain on the way of scientific inquiry.

[255] But this hope is very deceptive, for if cultivated reason can accomplish nothing with reference to the knowledge of certain things, the uncultivated will undoubtedly succeed as little. In metaphysics the appeal to the decisions of common sense is altogether inadmissible, since in this science no case can be presented *in concreto*. With morals, indeed, it is otherwise. Not only can all rules in morals be given *in concreto*, but practical reason reveals itself more clearly and correctly through the organ of common sense than through that of the speculative employment of the understanding. Hence common sense often judges more correctly about matters of morality and duty than the speculative understanding.

(*c*) *The Prejudice of Authority of the Age.*—Here the prejudice in favour of antiquity is one of the most important. Indeed we have good reason to judge favourably of antiquity; but that is only a reason for a moderate esteem, the limits of which we

overstep only too often by making the ancients the treasurers
of knowledge and sciences, elevating the *relative* value of their
writings to an *absolute*, and trusting ourselves blindly to their
guidance. To value the ancients so extravagantly is to bring
back the understanding to its period of childhood, and to neglect the employment of our own talents. We should also err
very much if we believed that all the ancients wrote as classi-
cally as those whose writings have come down to us. In fact,
as time sifts everything, and only that survives which has an
intrinsic value, we may assume, not without reason, that we
possess only the best writings of the ancients.

[256] There are several causes which produce and maintain
the prejudice of antiquity.

When anything surpasses our expectation based on a general
rule, then at first we *wonder* at it, and this wonder often passes
into admiration. This is the case with the ancients when we
find something in them which, having regard to the circumstances of the time in which they lived, we did not look for.
Another cause lies in the circumstance that knowledge of the
ancients and antiquity is a proof of learning and extensive
reading which always command respect, however common and
insignificant in themselves the things may be that we have
drawn from the study of the ancients. A third cause is the
gratitude we owe to the ancients because they have opened the
way to many branches of knowledge. It seems only fair to
show them a specially high esteem on this account, the measure
of which, however, we often overstep. Lastly, a fourth cause
is to be found in a certain *jealousy* of our contemporaries. The
man that is unable to compete with his contemporaries extols
the ancients at their expense, in order that the moderns may not
be able to elevate themselves above him.

The opposite of this is the prejudice of novelty. At certain
periods the authority of antiquity and the prejudice in its favour fell off, especially at the beginning of this century, when
the celebrated Fontenelle threw himself on the side of the
moderns. In those branches of knowledge that are capable of

extension it is very natural that we should place more confidence in the moderns than in the ancients. [257] But this judgment, also, is only justified as a provisional judgment. If we make it definite it becomes a prejudice.

2°. *Prejudices from Self-love or Logical Egoism*, by which a man holds that the agreement of his own judgment with that of others may be dispensed with as a criterion of truth. These are opposed to the prejudices of authority, as they [show] themselves in a certain predilection for an external thing which is the product of our own understanding, *ex. gr.* our own system.

Is it good and advisable to allow prejudices to remain, or even to favour them? It is astonishing that in our age such questions can still be proposed, especially that relating to the favouring of prejudices. To favour a person's prejudices means just with kind intent to deceive a person. But it may be permitted to leave prejudices unattacked, for who can make it his business to detect and remove the prejudices of everybody? Whether it is not advisable, however, to labour with all our power to eradicate them, this is a different question. Old and deep-rooted prejudices are indeed hard to combat, because they defend themselves, and are as it were their own judges. It is also sought to excuse the allowing prejudices to remain on the ground that disadvantages would arise from their removal. But even admitting these disadvantages, they will in the end produce the more good.

[258] X.

PROBABILITY — DEFINITION OF PROBABILITY — DISTINCTION BE-
TWEEN PROBABILITY AND VERISIMILITUDE — MATHEMATICAL
AND PHILOSOPHICAL PROBABILITY — DOUBT, SUBJECTIVE AND
OBJECTIVE — SCEPTICAL, DOGMATICAL, AND CRITICAL METHOD
OF PHILOSOPHIZING — HYPOTHESES.

To the doctrine of the certainty of our knowledge belongs
also the doctrine of the knowledge of the probable, which is to
be regarded as an approximation to certainty.

By probability we are to understand an assent from inadequate reasons, which however bear a greater proportion to the
adequate reasons than do the reasons for the opposite. By this
definition we distinguish probability (*probabilitas*) from mere
verisimilitude (*verisimilitudo*), which is an assent from inadequate reasons in so far as these are greater than the reasons for
the opposite.

For the ground of assent may be either *objectively* or *subjectively* greater than that of the opposite. Which of the two it
is can only be discovered by comparing the reasons of assent
with adequate reasons, for, when adequate, the reasons for assent
are greater than those for the opposite *can be*. In the case of
probability, then, the ground of assent is *objectively valid;* in that
of verisimilitude it is only *subjectively valid.* Verisimilitude is
only strength of persuasion ; probability is an approximation to
certainty. In probability there must always exist a standard
by which I can estimate it. This standard is certainty. For
as I have to compare inadequate with adequate reasons, I must
know what is required for certainty. [259] Such a standard,
however, does not exist in the case of mere verisimilitude ; since
in this I do not compare the inadequate reasons with adequate,
but with the reasons for the opposite.

The elements of probability may be either *homogeneous* or
heterogeneous. If they are homogeneous, as in mathematical
knowledge, they must be *numbered;* if heterogeneous, as in

philosophical knowledge, they must be *weighed*, that is, estimated by their effect, and this by the conquest of hindrances in the mind. The latter give no proportion to certainty, but only that of one verisimilitude to another. Hence it follows that it is only the mathematician that can determine the proportion of inadequate to adequate reasons ; the philosopher must be satisfied with verisimilitude, an assent only subjectively and practically adequate. For in philosophical questions, on account of the heterogeneity of the reasons, the probability cannot be estimated—the weights in this case are, so to speak, not stamped. It is therefore only of *mathematical* probability that we can properly say, that *it is more than half certainty.*

Much has been said of a logic of probability (*logica probabilium*). But this is not possible ; for if the proportion of the inadequate to adequate reasons cannot be mathematically estimated, no rules will be of any use. Nor can we give any general rules of probability except that error is not to be found all on one side, but there must be some ground of agreement in the object; and secondly, that when there are errors on *two opposite sides* in the same *number* and *degree*, then the truth lies in the *middle.*

[260] *Doubt* is a counter reason, or a mere hindrance to assent, and may be considered either *subjectively* or *objectively*. *Subjectively* doubt is sometimes taken to mean an undecided state of mind; and *objectively* the recognition of the insufficiency of the reasons for assent. In the latter respect it is called an Objection, that is, an objective reason for regarding as false a cognition held to be true.

A merely subjectively valid reason against assent is a scruple. In the case of a scruple we do not know whether the obstacle to assent is objective or only subjective, having its foundation, for example, only in inclination, custom, &c. A man may doubt without definitely and distinctly explaining to himself the ground of his doubt, and without being able to discern whether this ground is in the object itself or only in the subject. Now in order that such scruples should be removed, they must be raised to the distinctness and definiteness of an objection. For by means of objections certainty is brought to distinctness and completeness, and no one can be certain of a thing unless counter reasons are stirred by means of which it can be determined how far one is still removed from certainty, or how near one is to it. Nor is it enough that each doubt should merely be answered, it must also be *solved*, that is, we must make it comprehensible how the scruple has originated. If this is not done, the doubt is only *rejected*, not *removed;* the seed of the doubt still remains. In many cases, indeed, we cannot know whether the obstacle to assent in us has only subjective or objective grounds, so that we cannot remove the scruple by detecting the semblance, since we cannot always compare our cognitions with the object, but often only with one another. It is therefore the part of modesty to put forward our objections only as doubts.

[261] There is one principle of doubting which consists in the maxim to treat cognitions with the view of making them uncertain, and of showing the impossibility of attaining certainty. This method of philosophizing is the sceptical tone or Scepticism. It is opposed to the dogmatic tone or Dogmatism, which is a blind confidence in the power of reason to extend itself *a priori* by means of mere concepts without critical examination, and this merely on account of the apparent success of the method.

Both methods, if adopted universally, are fallacious. For there are many cognitions with respect to which we cannot proceed dogmatically; and on the other side as scepticism renounces all affirmative knowledge, it destroys all our exertions to attain the possession of a knowledge of what is certain.

Mischievous, however, as this scepticism is, yet the sceptical *method* is useful and judicious, if by this we understand nothing more than the method of treating a thing as uncertain, and bringing it to the utmost degree of uncertainty in the hope of coming on the trace of truth by this path. This method is properly only a suspension of judgment. It is extremely useful to the *critical* process, by which is to be understood that method of philosophizing by which we examine the *sources* of our affirmations, objections, and the grounds on which these rest—a method which gives hope of attaining to certainty.

In mathematics and physics scepticism has no place. Only that branch of knowledge could have given occasion to it which is neither mathematical nor empirical—the *purely philosophical.* [262] Absolute scepticism declares that everything is semblance. It distinguishes, then, semblance from truth, and must therefore possess some mark of the distinction. Consequently it must suppose a knowledge of truth, and thereby it contradicts itself.

We remarked above with reference to probability that it is only an approximation to certainty. Now this is especially the case with hypotheses, by means of which we can never attain to apodictic certainty, but only to a degree of probability sometimes greater, sometimes less.

A Hypothesis is *an assent of the judgment to the truth of a principle on account of the sufficiency of the consequences;* or more briefly, *assent to a supposition as a principle.*

All assent, then, in the case of hypotheses is founded on this, that the supposition taken as a principle is adequate to explain other cognitions as consequences from it. For here we conclude from the truth of the consequence to the truth of the principle. But since this mode of inference, as we have already remarked, cannot supply an adequate criterion of truth, or lead to apodictic certainty, unless *all the possible* consequences of an assumed principle are true, hence it is clear that as we can never determine all possible consequences, hypotheses always remain hypotheses, that is, suppositions to the full certainty of which we can never attain.

Nevertheless, the probability of a hypothesis may increase and be raised to an *analogue* of certainty, namely, when all the consequences *which we have hitherto met with* can be explained from the supposed principle. For in such a case no reason exists why we should not assume that all possible consequences may be explained from it. [263] In this case, then, we accept the hypothesis as if it were perfectly certain, although it has only the certainty of induction.

Yet in every hypothesis there must be something apodictically certain, viz.: First—*The possibility of the supposition itself.* For instance, when we assume a subterranean fire for the purpose of explaining earthquakes and volcanoes, such a fire must be possible, if not as a flaming, yet as a hot body. But for the sake of explaining certain other phenomena, to make the earth an animal in which the circulation of the internal juices produces heat, is to put forward a mere fiction, and not a hypothesis; for actualities may be invented but not possibilities—these must be certain.

Secondly—The consequence. The results must follow legitimately from the assumed principle, otherwise the hypothesis becomes a mere chimera.

Thirdly—Unity. It is an essential requirement of a hypothesis that it be only one, not needing any subsidiary hypothesis to support it. If in the case of a hypothesis we are obliged to adopt several others to help it out, it thereby loses very much of its probability. For the more consequences can be derived from a hypothesis, so much the more probable it is; the fewer, the more improbable. Thus, for instance, the hypothesis of Tycho Brahe is not sufficient to explain several phenomena; hence he was obliged to complete it by assuming several new hypotheses. Here, then, clearly we may guess that the assumed hypothesis cannot be the true principle. On the other hand the Copernican system is a hypothesis from which everything may be explained that ought to be explained by it *so far as has yet been observed.* Here we do not require any subsidiary hypotheses (*hypotheses subsidiariæ*).

[264] There are sciences that do not admit hypotheses, *ex. gr.* mathematics and metaphysics. But in natural philosophy they are useful and indispensable.

APPENDIX.

OF THE DISTINCTION BETWEEN THEORETICAL AND PRACTICAL KNOWLEDGE.

A cognition is called *practical* in contrast to *theoretical*, and also to *speculative* cognitions. Practical cognitions are either—

1°. Imperatives, and these are opposed to theoretical cognitions ; or,

2°. They contain *the principles of possible imperatives*, and are then opposed to speculative cognitions.

By imperative is to be understood every proposition that expresses a possible free action by which a certain end is to be attained. Every cognition, then, that contains imperatives is practical, and is so called in contrast to theoretical cognitions. For theoretical cognitions are those which express not what ought to be, but what is ; and therefore have as their object not an *action* but a *fact*.

If, on the other hand, we contrast practical cognitions with *speculative*, the former may themselves be *theoretical, provided only that imperatives can be derived from them.* Considered in this respect they are *potentially (in potentia)* or *objectively* practical. For by speculative cognitions we understand those from which no rules of conduct can be derived, or which contain no principles of possible imperatives. [265] A great number of such speculative propositions occur, *ex. gr.* in theology. Such speculative cognitions, therefore, are always theoretical ; but it is not true conversely that every theoretical cognition is speculative ; it may possibly, from another point of view, be practical also.

Everything in the end verges towards the *practical*, and it is in this tendency of all theory and all speculation in reference to their employment that the practical value of our knowledge consists. This value, however, is not *unconditional*, unless the *end* to which the practical employment of the cognition is directed is an *unconditional* end. The only unconditional and final end (ultimate end) to which all practical employment of our knowledge must ultimately refer is Morality, which for this reason we call the *absolutely practical*. And that part of philosophy which treats of morality must therefore be called practical philosophy, κατ᾽ ἐξοχήν ; although every other philosophical science may also have its *practical* part, that is, may contain, drawn from the theories set forth, a direction for the practical employment of them for the realization of certain ends.

THE MISTAKEN SUBTILTY OF THE FOUR SYLLOGISTIC
FIGURES.

(FIRST PUBLISHED, 1762.)

SECTION I.

General Conception of the Nature of Ratiocination.

Judgment is the comparison of a thing with some mark [or
attribute]. The thing itself is the Subject, the mark [or attri-
bute] is the Predicate. The comparison is expressed by the
word " is," which when used alone indicates that the predicate
is a mark [or attribute] of the subject, but when combined with
the sign of negation states that the predicate is a mark opposed
to the subject. In the former case the judgment is affirmative,
in the latter negative. It is readily understood that in calling
the predicate a mark [or attribute] we do not thereby say that
it is a mark of the subject, for this is the case only in affirmative judgments, but that it is regarded as a mark [or attribute]
of something, although in a negative judgment it contradicts
the subject. Thus let " a spirit " be the thing of which I
think ; " compounded " an attribute of something ; the judgment " a spirit is not compounded," represents this attribute as
inconsistent with the thing.

The mark of a mark [attribute of an attribute] of a thing is
called a "mediate mark " [or attribute] of the thing. Thus
" necessary " is an immediate attribute of God, but " unchangeable " is an attribute of what is necessary, and is therefore a
mediate attribute of God. It is easily seen that the immediate
attribute occupies the position of an intermediate mark [or at-
tribute] (*nota intermedia*) between the more remote one and the
thing itself, [58] since it is only by means of it that the remote

attribute is compared with the thing itself. But we can also compare an attribute with a thing negatively by means of an intermediate attribute, namely, by recognising that something is inconsistent with the immediate attribute of a thing. Thus, " contingent," as an attribute, is inconsistent with " necessary ;" but " necessary " is an attribute of God ; and thus by means of an intermediate attribute we recognise that contingency is inconsistent with God.

Now, then, I establish my real definition of *Ratiocination. Every judgment by means of a mediate attribute is a Ratiocination ;* or, in other words, it is the comparison of an attribute with a thing by means of an intermediate attribute. This intermediate attribute (*nota intermedia*) in a rational inference is also called the middle term (*terminus medius*) ; what the other terms are is sufficiently known.

In order to recognise clearly the relation of the attribute to the thing in the judgment—" the human soul is a spirit "—I avail myself of the intermediate attribute, " rational," so that by means of it I regard " being a spirit," as a mediate attribute of the human soul. There must necessarily be three judgments here, viz.—

1. Being a spirit is a mark [or attribute] of what is rational ;
2. Rational is a mark [or attribute] of the human soul ;
3. Being a spirit is a mark [or attribute] of the human soul ;

for the comparison of a remote attribute with the thing itself is only possible by these three operations.

Stated in the form of judgments they would stand thus : Everything rational is a spirit ; the soul of man is rational ; consequently the soul of man is a spirit. This is an affirmative *ratiocination.* [59] As to the negative, it is equally obvious that since I cannot always recognise clearly enough the inconsistency of a predicate and subject, I must, if possible, avail myself of the aid of an intermediate attribute. Suppose there is proposed to me the judgment : the duration of God cannot be measured by any time, and that I do not find that this predicate compared thus directly with the subject gives me a sufficiently clear idea of the inconsistency, I avail myself of an attribute which I can immediately represent to myself in this subject, and I compare the predicate herewith, and by help of it with the thing itself. " Being measurable by time " is inconsistent with everything that is " unchangeable," but " unchangeable" is an attribute of God, therefore, &c. Formally expressed, this would stand thus : Nothing unchangeable is measureable by time ; the duration of God is unchangeable ; consequently, &c.

Section II.

Of the Supreme Rules of all Ratiocination.

From what has been said we see that the first and universal rule of all affirmative ratiocination is, *An attribute of an attribute is an attribute of the thing itself* [or : *A mark of a mark is a mark of the thing itself*] (*nota notæ est etiam nota rei ipsius*) ; that of all negative ratiocination, *whatever is inconsistent with the attribute* [*or mark*] *of a thing is inconsistent with the thing itself* (*repugnans notæ repugnat rei ipsi*). Neither of these rules is capable of proof. For a proof is only possible by means of one or more rational inferences ; hence an attempt to prove the supreme formula of all ratiocination would be to reason in a circle. But that these rules contain the universal and ultimate ground of every kind of ratiocination is clear from this, that those rules which have hitherto been regarded by all logicians as the first rules of all ratiocination must borrow the sole ground of their truth from our rule. [60] *The dictum de omni*, the supreme principle of affirmative syllogisms, is expressed thus : Whatever is universally affirmed of a concept is also affirmed of everything

contained under it. The proof of this is clear. The concept which
contains others under it has always been abstracted from them
as an attribute : now whatever belongs to this concept is an attribute of an attribute, and hence is also an attribute of the things
themselves from which it has been abstracted, that is, it belongs
to the lower concepts which are contained under it. Everyone
who is even slightly instructed in logical matters will see at
once that this *Dictum* is true only for this reason, and that
therefore it is subordinate to our rule. The *Dictum de nullo*
stands in the same relation to our second rule. Whatever is
universally denied of a concept is also denied of everything that
is contained under it. For the concept under which these others
are contained is merely an attribute abstracted from them. Now
whatever is inconsistent with this attribute is inconsistent with
the thing itself ; consequently, whatever is inconsistent with
the higher concepts must also be inconsistent with the lower
which are contained under it.

Section III.

Of Pure and Mixed Ratiocination.

Everyone knows that there are immediate inferences, since
from the truth of one judgment that of another may be discerned immediately without any middle term. On this account
inferences of this kind are not Ratiocinations. For example,
from the proposition : all matter is changeable, follows at once :
whatever is not changeable is not matter. Logicians enumerate
different kinds of these immediate inferences ; amongst which
undoubtedly that by logical conversion, and that by contraposition, are the most important.

[61] Now when a ratiocination takes place by means of three
propositions only ; according to the rules which have just been

stated for all ratiocination, I call this a *pure ratiocination* (*ratiocinium purum*); if, however, it is only possible by a combination of more than three judgments it is a mixed ratiocination (*ratiocinium hybridum*). Suppose, namely, that between the three main propositions there must be interposed an immediate inference from one of them, so that there is a proposition more than a pure ratiocination admits, then we have a *ratiocinium hybridum*. For example, suppose one should argue thus:

Nothing that is corruptible is simple,
Hence, nothing simple is corruptible ;
The soul of man is simple,
Therefore the soul of man is not corruptible,

we would not, indeed, be employing a compound ratiocination properly so-called, since this would consist of several ratiocinations ; whereas this contains, in addition to what is required in a single ratiocination, one more immediate inference by contraposition, thus containing four propositions.

Even if, however, only three judgments are expressed, yet if the sequence of the conclusion from these judgments be possible only by the help of a legitimate logical conversion, contraposition, or some other logical alteration of one of these judgments, the ratiocination would still be a *ratiocinium hybridum ;* for the question is not what is said, but what it is indispensably necessary to think, in order that there may be a valid sequence. Suppose that in the ratiocination

Nothing corruptible is simple,
The soul of man is simple,
Therefore, the soul of man is not corruptible,

the sequence is valid only provided that by a valid conversion of the major I can say : [62] Nothing corruptible is simple, consequently nothing simple is corruptible; then the ratiocination is still mixed, because its validity rests on the latent insertion of this immediate consequence, which one must have at least in thought.

Section IV.

*In the so-called First Figure Pure Ratiocinations only are possible,
in the remaining Figures only mixed.*

When a Ratiocination is conducted immediately according to
one of our two rules above stated, then it is always in the first
figure. The first rule runs thus : An attribute B of an attribute C of a thing A is an attribute of the thing A itself.
Hence arise three propositions :—

	C B
C has the attribute B,	What is rational is a spirit,
	A C
A has the attribute C,	The human soul is rational,
	A B
Therefore, A has the attribute B.	Therefore the human soul is a spirit.

It is easy to give many similar instances and others to which
the rule of negative reasonings applies, so as to convince oneself that whenever the reasonings conform to these rules they
stand in the first figure; and I may justly avoid such tedious
detail. It is readily perceived that these rules of ratiocinations
do not require that besides these judgments any immediate inference from one or other proposition should be interpolated in
order that the argument should be valid ; hence, the ratiocination in the first figure is of the pure kind.

[63] *In the Second Figure only mixed Ratiocinations are possible.*

The rule of the Second Figure is this : Whatever is inconsistent with the attribute of a thing is inconsistent with the
thing itself.

This is true only because that with which an attribute is
inconsistent is also inconsistent with this attribute, and whatever is inconsistent with an attribute is inconsistent with the

thing itself; therefore that with which an attribute of a thing is inconsistent is inconsistent with the thing itself.

Here now it is manifest that it is only because I can simply convert the major as a [universal] negative, that an inference by means of the minor to the conclusion is possible. Hence, I must have covertly performed this conversion in thought, else my premisses would not be conclusive. But the proposition resulting from this conversion is an interpolated immediate inference from the first premiss, and the ratiocination has four judgments, and is a *ratiocinium hybridum*. For instance, if I say

> No spirit is divisible,
> All matter is divisible,
> Consequently, no matter is a spirit,

my inference is valid; only the force of it lies in this, that from the first premiss "no spirit is divisible," follows by immediate inference; consequently, "nothing divisible is a spirit," and by this the whole inference proceeds correctly according to the universal rule of all ratiocination. But inasmuch as it is only by virtue of this immediate inference therefrom that there is a *vis consequentiæ* in the argument, this inference really belongs to it, and it has four judgments:

> No spirit is divisible,
> And therefore nothing divisible is a spirit;
> All matter is divisible,
> Therefore no matter is a spirit.

[64] *In the Third Figure none but mixed Ratiocinations are possible.*

The rule of the Third Figure is the following: Whatever belongs to or contradicts a thing, also belongs to or contradicts some things that are contained under another attribute of this thing. Now this proposition itself is true only because I can (*per conversionem logicam*) convert the judgment in which it is said that another attribute belongs to the thing, by which

means it becomes conformable to the rule of all ratiocination.
For instance :

> All men are sinners,
> All men are rational,
> Therefore, some rational beings are sinners.

This follows only because by conversion (*per accidens*) I can
argue thus from the minor ; consequently some rational beings
are men, and then the concepts are compared according to the
rule of all ratiocination, but only by means of the interpolation
of an immediate inference ; and thus we have a *ratiocinium
hybridum :*

> All men are sinners,
> All men are rational,
> Hence, some rational beings are men,
> Therefore, some rational beings are sinners.

The same thing may be easily shown in the negative mode of
this figure, which I omit for the sake of brevity.

*In the Fourth Figure none but mixed Ratiocinations are pos-
sible.*

The mode of reasoning in the Fourth Figure is so unnatural,
and rests on so many intermediate inferences which must be
regarded as interpolated, that the rule which I might lay down
as universally applicable to it would be very obscure and unin-
telligible. [65] Therefore I will only state on what conditions
there is a valid inference in it. In the negative modes of this
figure a legitimate inference is possible only because I can change
the place of the extremes either by logical conversion or contraposition, and thus after each premiss can think its immediate
consequence, so that these consequences have the relation which
they ought to have in a ratiocination according to the general
rule. As to affirmative modes, I will show that they are not
possib'e in the fourth figure at all. Negative ratiocination in

this figure, as it must properly be conceived, will appear as follows :

> No stupid man is learned,
> Consequently, no learned person is stupid ;
> Some learned persons are pious,
> Consequently, some pious persons are learned,
> Therefore, some pious persons are not stupid.

Let the syllogism be of the second kind :

> Every spirit is simple ;
> Everything simple is incorruptible,
> Therefore something incorruptible is a spirit.

Here it is quite obvious that the conclusion as it stands cannot be derived from the premisses at all. This will be seen at once by comparing it with the middle term. In fact, I cannot say something incorruptible is a spirit, because it is simple ; for from the fact that something is simple it does not follow that it is a spirit. Moreover, the premisses cannot by any possible logical changes be so arranged that the conclusion, or another proposition from which it is an immediate consequence, could be derived from them, that is to say, if the extremes are to be placed according to the established rule in all figures so that the major term shall occur in the major premiss, the minor in the minor.[1] [66] And although by completely changing the places of the extremes, so that what was previously the major becomes the minor, and *vice versa*, a conclusion can be deduced from which the given conclusion follows, yet in that case a complete transposition of the premisses is necessary, and thus the so-called ratiocination in the fourth figure contains indeed the matter, but not the

---

[1] This rule is founded on the synthetical order by which first the more remote attribute [or mark] and then the reason is compared with the subject. Although this may be regarded as purely arbitrary, yet it becomes indispensably necessary if we choose to have four figures. For if it is indifferent whether I bring the predicate of the conclusion into the major premiss or the minor, then there is no difference between the first figure and the fourth. There is an error of this kind in Crusius' *Logic*, p. 600.

form of our reasoning, and is not at all a ratiocination according to the logical order in which alone the division of the four figures is possible. It is quite otherwise with the negative reasoning in this figure. The reasoning above given must in fact stand thus:

> Every spirit is simple,
> Everything simple is incorruptible,
> Therefore, every spirit is incorruptible,
> Hence, something incorruptible is a spirit.

This is quite legitimate, but argument of this kind is not distinguished from one in the first figure by a difference in the place of the middle term, but only by this, that the order of the premisses has been changed, and in the conclusion the order of the extremes.[1] [67] But this does not constitute an alteration in the figure. There is an error of this kind in Crusius' *Logic* in the place referred to, where the author believes that by taking the liberty of changing the order of the premisses he draws the conclusion in the fourth figure, and that more naturally. It is a pity to see the trouble that an able man takes trying to improve a useless thing. The only useful thing one can do with it is to annihilate it.

---

[1] For if the premiss which contains the predicate of the conclusion is the major premiss, then in relation to the real conclusion which follows immediately from the premisses, the second premiss is the major, and the first is the minor. But then everything proceeds according to the first figure, only that the proposed conclusion is drawn by logical conversion from the conclusion which follows directly from the aforesaid judgments.

Section V.

The Logical Division of the Four Figures is a Mistaken Subtilty.

It cannot be denied that we can draw conclusions legitimately in all these figures. But it is incontestable that all
except the first determine the conclusion only by a roundabout
way, and by interpolated inferences, and that the very same
conclusion would follow from the same middle term in the first
figure by pure and unmixed reasoning. It might then be
thought that the other three figures were at worst useless, but
not false. But when we consider the purpose for which they
were invented, and for which they are still expounded, we shall
come to a different conclusion. If what we wanted were to entangle the principal judgments with a multitude of inferences
mingled with them in such a way that, some being expressed
and some suppressed, it should require much art to judge of
their agreement with the rules of inference, we should be able
to invent not indeed more figures, but more enigmatical argu-
ments, which might give plenty of brain-worry. But it is not
the purpose of Logic to entangle, but to disentangle; to set
forth something not in a covert but in an open fashion. Therefore these four kinds of reasoning ought to be simple, unmixed,
and without concealed bye-inferences, otherwise they cannot be
permitted to appear in a logical treatise as formulæ giving the
clearest representation of an argument. [68] It is also certain
that hitherto all logicians have regarded them as simple ratiocinations not requiring the interposition of other judgments,
otherwise they would never have conceded to them this privilege. The three latter figures then, regarded as rules of
ratiocination, are no doubt correct; but regarded as containing
a simple and pure reasoning, they are incorrect. This in-
correctness, which claims the right of entangling knowledge,
whereas the proper object of Logic is to bring everything to

the simplest mode of cognition, is so much the greater, as special rules are necessary for each figure in order to avoid tripping in thus swerving from the path. In truth, if there ever was a case in which much acuteness has been applied, and much apparent learning wasted on an utterly useless thing, it is this. The so-called moods which are possible in each figure, indicated by strange words, which also with much mysterious art contain letters to facilitate the change to the first figure, will hereafter be valued as a curiosity in the history of the human mind, when the venerable rust of antiquity shall teach a better instructed posterity to admire and deplore the toilsome and fruitless labours of their ancestors as exhibited in these relics.

It is easy, moreover, to discover what gave the first occasion of this subtilty. The man who first having written a syllogism in three successive lines, looked on it as a chessboard, and tried to find what would come out of a change in the place of the middle term, was surprised to find that a rational meaning always emerged, just as one is surprised at finding an anagram in a name. [69] It was as childish to be delighted with the one as with the other, especially as it was forgotten that nothing new in point of clearness was produced, but only an increase of obscurity. But indeed this is the lot of the human understanding : either it is subtle and falls into distortions, or it vainly tries to grasp too great objects and builds castles in the air. In the great crowd of thinkers one chooses the number 666, another the origin of animals and plants, or the secrets of Providence. The error into which both fall is of very different fashion as the minds are different.

The number of things worthy of being known is much increased in our times. By-and-by our capacity will be too weak and our life too short to grasp only the most useful part of them. There is riches in abundance, to obtain which we must throw away again much useless lumber. It would have been better never to have burdened oneself with it.

I do not flatter myself so much as to suppose that the work

of a few hours will be sufficient to overthrow the colossus which hides its head in the clouds of antiquity, and whose feet are of clay. My purpose is only to explain why in my lectures on Logic, in which I cannot arrange everything according to my own view, but must do much in conformity with the prevailing fashion, I shall be brief in these matters in order to spend the time gained thereby in the actual enlargement of profitable knowledge.

There is another use of syllogistic, namely, that it enables one in a learned dispute to vanquish an incautious adversary. But as this only belongs to the athletics of the learned, an art which, however useful it may be otherwise, does not contribute much to the advancement of truth, I pass it over in silence.

---

[70] Section VI.

Concluding Observation.

We learn then that the supreme rules of all ratiocinations lead directly to that order of the terms which is called the first figure ; that all other displacements of the middle term yield a correct inference only because they lead by easy immediate inferences to such propositions as are connected in the simple order of the first figure ; that it is impossible to draw simple and unmixed inferences in more than one figure, since the *vis consequentiæ* is still only in the first figure, which by help of covert inferences lies hidden in a ratiocination, and the altered position of the terms only makes it necessary to proceed by a more or less roundabout way in order to see the consequence ; and thus we see that the division of the figures, if they are intended to contain pure inferences unmixed with interpolated judgments, is mistaken and impossible. It is easy to see from our explanation how our universal fundamental rules of all ratiocination contain the special rules of the so-called first figure, and also how with the given conclusion and the middle term we can change every argument in one of the other figures into the first and simple form without the useless tediousness of the formulæ of Reduction, so that either the very conclusion itself shall be drawn, or one from which it follows by immediate inference. I need not then dwell on this point.

I will not conclude this observation without adding a few remarks which may be of considerable use at some other time.

[71] I say then, first, that a *distinct* concept is possible only by means of a *judgment*, a *complete* concept only by means of a *ratiocination*. In fact, in order that a concept should be distinct, I must clearly recognise something as an attribute of a thing, and this is a judgment. In order to have a distinct concept of body I clearly represent to myself impenetrability as an attribute of it. Now this representation is nothing but the thought "a body is impenetrable." Here it is to be observed that this judgment is not the distinct concept itself, but is the act by which it is realised; for the idea of the thing which arises after this act is distinct. It is easy to show that a complete concept is only possible by means of a ratiocination: for this it is sufficient to refer to the first section of this essay. We might say, therefore, that a distinct concept is one which is made clear by a judgment, and a complete concept one which is made distinct by a ratiocination. If the completeness is of the first degree, the ratiocination is simple, if of the second or third degree, it is only possible by means of a chain of reasoning which the understanding abridges in the manner of a Sorites. From this it is clear that in the ordinary treatment of Logic there is a serious error, in that distinct and complete concepts are treated before judgments and ratiocinations, although the former are only possible by means of the latter.

Secondly, as it is quite evident that the completeness of a concept and its distinctness do not require different faculties of the mind (since the same capacity which recognises something immediately as an attribute in a thing is also employed to recognise in this attribute another attribute, and thus to conceive the thing by means of a remote attribute), so also it is evident that Understanding and Reason, that is, the power of cognising distinctly, and the power of forming ratiocinations, are not different faculties. [72] Both possess the power of judging; but when we judge mediately we reason.

Thirdly, we may also conclude that the higher faculty of knowledge rests simply on the power of judging. Therefore, if a being can judge it possesses the higher capacity of knowledge. If we find reason to deny it this latter, then neither can it judge. The neglect of such considerations has led a celebrated writer to attribute to the lower animals distinct concepts. An ox, says he, in his conception of the stable, has also a clear conception of its attribute [or mark] the door, and therefore has a distinct conception of the stable. It is easy to detect the confusion here. The distinctness of a concept does not consist in this, that something which is an attribute [or mark] of the thing is clearly represented, but that it is clearly cognised *as* an attribute [or mark] of the thing. The door, indeed, belongs to the stable, and may serve as the attribute [or mark] of it; but it is only he who frames the judgment, "This door belongs to this stable," that has a distinct concept of the building, and this is certainly beyond the power of the beast.

I go still further, and say, it is quite a different thing to *distinguish* things from one another, and to *cognise* the *distinction* of things. The latter is only possible by means of judgments, and cannot be accomplished by an irrational animal. The following distinction may be of great use: *Logical distinction* is the cognition that a thing A is not B, and is always a negative judgment. To distinguish physically is to be impelled by different ideas to different actions.

[73] The dog distinguishes roast meat from bread because he is affected differently by them (for different things produce different sensations), and the sensation of the former is the

source of a different desire in him from that of the latter, in consequence of the natural connexion of his instincts and his ideas.[1] From this we draw the suggestion to study more carefully the essential distinction between rational and irrational animals. If we could discover what that secret faculty is by which judgment is possible, we should solve the difficulty. My present opinion inclines to this, that this faculty or capacity is nothing but the power of the internal sense, that is, the power of making our own ideas the object of our thoughts. This power cannot be derived from any other; it is a fundamental faculty in the proper sense of the word, and as I hold, can belong to rational beings only. And the whole of the higher faculty of knowledge rests on the same power. I conclude with a remark which must please those who can feel pleasure in observing the unity in human cognitions. All affirmative judgments come under one common formula, the principle of Identity, *cuilibet subjecto competit prædicatum ipsi identicum;* all negative judgments under the principle of Contradiction, *nulli subjecto competit prædicatum ipsi oppositum.* All affirmative ratiocinations are contained under the rule, [74] *nota notæ est nota rei ipsius;* all negative ratiocinations under this, *oppositum notæ opponitur rei ipsi.* All judgments which come immediately under the principles of Identity or of Contradiction, that is, in which the identity or the contradiction is discerned not by means of an intermediate attribute (and therefore not by analysis of the concepts), but immediately, are unprovable judgments; those judgments in which the identity or contradiction is mediately cognisable are provable. Human knowledge is full of such unprovable judgments. Some of these come before every definition, since in order to arrive at

---

[1] It is in fact of the greatest importance to attend to this in an inquiry into the nature of the lower animals. In observing them we are aware merely of certain outward actions, the difference of which indicates a difference in the determinations of their desire. But it by no means follows that this is preceded in them by such an act of the faculty of knowledge that they are conscious of the agreement or disagreement of what is contained in one sensation with what is contained in another.

the definition we must represent to ourselves as an attribute of a thing that which we in the first instance immediately recognise in the thing   Those philosophers are mistaken who proceed as if there were no fundamental truths incapable of proof except a simple one.   Those are equally mistaken who are too free in admitting several of their propositions to this privilege without sufficient guarantee.

NOTES BY COLERIDGE.

PAGE 27.

" The principles (as it were, the supporting skeleton) of beauty rest on *a priori* laws no less than Logic. The *kind* is constituted by laws inherent in the reason; it is the *degree*, that which enriches the *formalis* into the *formosum*, that calls in the aid of the senses. And even this, the sensuous and sensual ingredient, must be an analogue to the former. It is not every agreeable that can form a component part of beauty."

PAGE 45, LINE 7.

" Is the understanding then (Verstand) a separate agent from the man himself? How much more easy it would be to say that man errs not by the imperfection but by the misuse or non-exertion of his faculties. But even this does not represent the case fully and fairly; for nature compels us in numberless instances to judge according to our present perceptions, modified by our past experience, and in these the limits and imperfections of our faculties are sometimes necessarily causes of erroneous judgments, for this plain reason, that the sense of outwardness as a sense of reality is a law of our nature, no conclusion of our judgment."

PAGE 72, PARAGRAPHS 2 and 3.

"This appears to be obscurely stated. I do not question its truth; but it requires much previous instruction and explanation to render it applicable. As it is here given it seems to be no more than that the Probable is differenced from the Plausible by superiority in the quality of the grounds; while the Plausible rests on the greater number or quantity. If so, the far simpler definition would be : the Probable is that which *is ;* the Plausible that which only *seems* likely. But at the best it is a mere verbal or dictionary definition, better suited to a Latin and English (or German) dictionary under the words Probabilis and Plausibilis. I see indeed what Kant meant, but I speak of the words in which his meaning is conveyed. But even with regard to the meaning, I cannot help suspecting that philosophic probability and the mathematical doctrine of chances are diverse, ἑτερογενῆ, and therefore incommensurable. The mathematical is useful *de quamplurimis* to the statesman whether of a kingdom, or of a life insurance association, and assumes that we know nothing *de singulis ;* hence the committees are obliged to recur to the philosophic probability in the admission of each member."

INDEX.

THE END.

INTRODU

IMMANUEL

ence